Working English

Englisch im Beruf

Phrase Book

LANGENSCHEIDT

BERLIN · MÜNCHEN · WIEN · ZÜRICH · NEW YORK

Working English
by
Paul Westlake
Eeva-Liisa Pitkänen
Eero Lehtonen
Kate Moore

Editor: Anita Seppovaara
Illustrations: Pertti Anikari
Photos: Eero Lehtonen, Riina Hyytiä, Paul Westlake
Design: Heikki Kalliomaa
Layout: Timo Lagerkrans, Eeva-Liisa Pitkänen
Editorial assistance: Paul Dillingham, Merja Hyytiäinen

Auflage:	7.	6.	5.	4.	Letzte Zahlen
Jahr:	2002	01	00	99	maßgeblich

Printed in Finland by WSOY.
ISBN 3-468-48826-2

WORKING ENGLISH

PHRASE BOOK

This pocket phrase book provides you with easy and instant access to a wide selection of modern English phrases for use in work situations.

German Key (p. 5)
provides you with a German–English list of language targets (for use with Target Index 1 or Phrase List 1).

Target Index 1 (p. 11)
represents a straightforward breakdown and index of the language targets.

Phrase List 1 (p. 30)
enables you to find a group of phrases relating to a particular language target.

Target Index 2 (p. 117)
lists the language targets that appear in Phrase List 2.

Phrase List 2 (p. 125)
follows the themes of the TV series and is intended for use with the WORKING ENGLISH Course Book.

"This is not what I ordered."

GERMAN KEY

This list comprises the most important language targets and functions that appear in the WORKING ENGLISH Phrase Book. To help you find the appropriate functions in Target Index 1 and Phrase List 1 we have listed them alphabetically in German.

A

ablehnen DECLINING, REJECTING, REFUSING
abschweifen DIGRESSING
abwägen BALANCING
akzeptieren ACCEPTING, AGREEING
anbieten OFFERING
anderer Meinung sein DISAGREEING
anders ausdrücken REPHRASING
Änderungen CHANGES
anfangen STARTING, OPENING
sich anmelden REGISTERING
annehmen ACCEPTING
j-n ansprechen APPROACHING
Antrag MOTION
antworten RESPONDING
anzweifeln CHALLENGING
Arbeitsplatz WORKPLACE
Argumente POINTS
Aufmerksamkeit ATTENTION
Ausflüchte machen AVOIDING
ausgleichen BALANCING
j-n ausrufen lassen PAGING
ausweichen AVOIDING

B

beenden CLOSING, FINISHING
beginnen STARTING
Begrüßung GREETING, WELCOMING
Beispiele EXAMPLES
benachrichtigen INFORMING
berichten REPORTING
berichtigen CORRECTING
beruhigen REASSURING
Beschwerde COMPLAINT
Bestätigung CONFIRMATION
Besucher GUESTS, VISITORS
betonen EMPHASIZING
Bewirtung DRINKS, EATING, RESTAURANT
sich beziehen auf REFERRING
bitten REQUESTING

D

danken THANKING
Diskussion DISCUSSION

E

einführen INTRODUCING
Einigkeit CONSENSUS
Einladungen INVITATIONS
einleiten INTRODUCING
sich eintragen REGISTERING
Empfang(ssekretärin) RECEPTIONIST
sich entschuldigen APOLOGIZING, EXCUSES
erklären EXPLAINING
erlauben GRANTING, PERMISSION
Erlaubnis PERMISSION

M

Meinungen OPINIONS

N

Nachricht MESSAGE
Nachrichten NEWS
Neuigkeiten NEWS

O

Ordnung bewahren KEEPING ORDER
Ort PLACE

P

Präsentation PRESENTING
Probleme PROBLEMS
Protokoll MINUTES
prüfen CHECKING

R

Reisen TRAVELLING
Restaurant EATING, RESTAURANT
richtigstellen CORRECTING
Richtungsangabe DIRECTIONS

S

Schluß machen CLOSING, FINISHING
Sicherheit CERTAINTY
Sitzung MEETING

T

Tagesordnung AGENDA
telefonieren TELEPHONING

Termine APPOINTMENTS

U

übereinstimmen AGREEING
nicht übereinstimmen DISAGREEING
umformulieren REPHRASING
Ungewißheit UNCERTAINTY
Unkenntnis IGNORANCE
Unterkunft ACCOMMODATION, HOTELS
Unwahrscheinlichkeit IMPROBABILITY
Unwissenheit IGNORANCE

V

sich verabschieden GOODBYE, LEAVING
verallgemeinern GENERALIZING
Vereinbarungen ARRANGEMENTS
Verhandlungen NEGOTIATIONS
verschieben POSTPONING
verweigern REFUSING
Vorbehalt RESERVATION
vorbringen INTRODUCING
Vorschlag PROPOSAL, SUGGESTION
Vorstellungen INTRODUCTIONS
Vorzug PREFERENCE

W

wählen VOTING
Wahrscheinlichkeit PROBABILITY
Wiederholung REPETITION
willkommen heißen WELCOMING, GREETING
Worterteilung FLOOR

Z

Zeit TIME
Zögern HESITATION
auf j-n zugehen APPROACHING
zusammenfassen SUMMARIZING
zustimmen AGREEING, ACCEPTING
Zweck PURPOSE
Zweifel DOUBT

"Could we look at it in another light?"

TARGET INDEX 1

QUESTIONS

Fragen

PHRASE LIST 1: TARGETS LISTED ALPHABETICALLY

A

ACCEPTING

– *accepting time and place*
- ❑ Fine with me.
- ❑ OK. Let's meet there.
- ❑ Suits me fine.
- ❑ I'll be there.
- ❑ I'll be waiting for you in / at ...
- ❑ Good. What time would be most suitable for you?
- ❑ Great. I'll come and pick you up at your hotel at ...

– *accepting suggestions*
- ❑ That's a good idea.
- ❑ All right.
- ❑ (It's) not a bad idea.
- ❑ Yes, I suppose we could.

– *accepting invitations*
- ❑ I'd love to.
- ❑ I'd be delighted to.
- ❑ Yes. I'd like to very much. Thanks.
- ❑ That's very kind of you. I'd like that very much.

- ❑ That would be very nice.
- ❑ Sounds like a great idea.

– *accepting drinks*

- ❑ Thank you very much. I'll have a ..., please.
- ❑ Thank you. What do you recommend?
- ❑ Thank you. I'll have a ...
- ❑ I'd love one.

– *accepting a compromise*

- ❑ Yes. I think that would be perfectly acceptable.
- ❑ We would have no objections to that.
- ❑ That seems to be a reasonable compromise.
- ❑ To meet you halfway on this, I think we could agree to your condition.

ACCOMMODATION

– *asking about hotel accommodation*

- ❑ Do you have any vacancies?
- ❑ I'd like to inquire about ...
- ❑ I'd like to make a reservation for ...
- ❑ I'd like to know the price of ...
- ❑ How much do you charge for a single / double room?
- ❑ Is breakfast included in the price?
- ❑ What credit cards do you take?

ADDING

– *adding*

- ❑ I must add that ...
- ❑ In addition ...
- ❑ Not only ... but ...
- ❑ Furthermore ... / Moreover ...

– *adding information*

- ❑ There are certain points you should bear in mind.
- ❑ If we look at it in another light ...
- ❑ There are other considerations ...
- ❑ I wonder if you've considered ...
- ❑ Seen from another angle, one could ...
- ❑ Let me elaborate ...
- ❑ I'll explain it in greater detail.

AGENDA

– *dealing with the agenda*

- ❑ Has everyone seen the agenda?
- ❑ Has everyone received a copy of the agenda?
- ❑ Before we begin, I would like to add an item to the agenda.
- ❑ Referring to the agenda ...
- ❑ I would like to delete item five from the agenda.
- ❑ The agenda has been adopted.

AGREEING

– *expressing strong agreement*

- ❑ I totally agree.
- ❑ I agree with you completely.
- ❑ I agree with you on that.
- ❑ That's exactly my opinion.
- ❑ I think you're right.
- ❑ I couldn't agree more.
- ❑ I'm all in favour of that.
- ❑ You're absolutely right.

– *expressing partial agreement*

- ❑ Well, I agree with you on the whole, but ...

- ❑ I agree in principle, but ...
- ❑ Although I agree with most of what you've said, I ...
- ❑ I find it difficult to agree with your point about ...
- ❑ By and large I would accept your views, but ...
- ❑ Well, to a certain extent I agree with you, but ...
- ❑ You have a point there, but ...
- ❑ I have some sympathy with your position, but ...
- ❑ I take your point, but ...
- ❑ I can see your point of view, but ...

– *agreeing on meeting later*

- ❑ All right. What time and where?
- ❑ Shall we say at seven in the lobby?
- ❑ Yes, I don't see why not.
- ❑ OK, seven it is then. See you later.

APOLOGIZING

– *apologizing*

- ❑ I'm terribly / awfully / really sorry, but I'm afraid ...
- ❑ Sorry about ...
- ❑ It's entirely our fault.
- ❑ Sorry about all this.
- ❑ Is there anything I can do?
- ❑ Please accept my apologies.
- ❑ I'm sorry. If there's anything I can do ...

APPOINTMENTS

– *making an appointment*

- ❑ I'd like to make an appointment with ...

- ❑ Would it be possible to make an appointment with ...?
- ❑ I was wondering if it would be possible to make an appointment with ...

– *informing reception of your arrival*

- ❑ I have an appointment with Mr / Ms ... at ...
- ❑ I'm here from ...
- ❑ My name is ... I'm here to see ...
- ❑ I'm ... Can you tell me where ... is, please?

APPROACHING

– *approaching others*

- ❑ Mr ... / Ms ....?
- ❑ It's ..., isn't it?
- ❑ Excuse me, are you ...?
- ❑ Hello, you must be ...

– *receiving a visitor (receptionist)*

- ❑ How can I help you?
- ❑ May I help you?
- ❑ What can I do for you?
- ❑ Can I help you?

ARRANGEMENTS

– *arranging time*

- ❑ Can we agree on a time?
- ❑ Shall we say ...?
- ❑ What day would be the most convenient for you?
- ❑ What day would suit you best?
- ❑ What time of day ...?
- ❑ How long do you think we'll need?
- ❑ When will you be arriving in ...?

– *arranging place*
- ❑ Where should we meet?
- ❑ Let's meet at ...
- ❑ What about if we meet at ...? / What about meeting at ...?
- ❑ I suggest we meet at ... / Why don't we meet at ...?
- ❑ What's the address?
- ❑ Do you know the address?
- ❑ Do you know how to get here?
- ❑ Should I take a cab / taxi?
- ❑ Shall I pick you up at ...?
- ❑ Just to make sure I've got the time and place right ...

– *making travel arrangements*
- ❑ I'd like to find out about ...
- ❑ Do you have any information on ...?
- ❑ I'm inquiring about ...
- ❑ I'd like a ... ticket to ..., please.
- ❑ Do I have to change?
- ❑ I'd like to make a reservation, please.
- ❑ Do you accept credit cards?
- ❑ I'd like to book a ...

– *making changes in travel arrangements*
- ❑ I'd like to make a change in my reservation.
- ❑ Is it possible to exchange this ticket for ...?
- ❑ I'd like to change my ...
- ❑ I'd like to cancel ...

– *inquiring about arrangements*
- ❑ I'd just like to know whether it's possible to ...
- ❑ Where do I sign up for ...?

- ❑ Where can I get ...?
- ❑ Who do I see to arrange ...?
- ❑ To whom do I talk to arrange ...?
- ❑ I need ... How can that be arranged?
- ❑ How can I get hold of ...?
- ❑ Where's ... being held?
- ❑ Can you tell me where ... is, please?

– *confirming arrangements*

- ❑ I'm phoning about ...
- ❑ I'd just like to make sure you've received our ...
- ❑ I just wanted to make sure everything's in order.
- ❑ You haven't made it clear to us ...
- ❑ Could you send us confirmation by fax, please?

– *informing someone about changes in schedule*

- ❑ The original schedule has been updated.
- ❑ There's a slight change in the schedule.
- ❑ The ... has been postponed until ...
- ❑ The room assignments have been changed.
- ❑ ..., scheduled to be held in ..., will now be meeting in ...
- ❑ Due to technical reasons the ... has been cancelled.
- ❑ Due to unforeseen circumstances ...
- ❑ Due to circumstances beyond our control ...
- ❑ Apologies from Mr / Ms ... Unfortunately he / she won't be able to participate.
- ❑ Before we begin, I would like to announce that ..., which means there's a slight change in the schedule.
- ❑ I think we must postpone ... until ...

❑ Mr / Ms ...'s presentation has been moved to ...

ASSISTANCE

– *offering assistance*

❑ Can I help you in some way?
❑ May I be of assistance?
❑ Would you like me to do it for you?
❑ Can I give you a hand?

– *asking for assistance*

❑ I wonder if you can help me.
❑ Do you think you could send this ... for me?
❑ Sorry to bother you, but would you mind ...?

– *thanking someone for assistance*

❑ Thank you very much (indeed) for your help.
❑ Thanks for your assistance.
❑ Thank you for helping me.
❑ I appreciate your help.
❑ Thank you. I'd appreciate it.

ATTENTION

– *drawing attention to a point*

❑ As you can see, ...
❑ As you have noticed, ...
❑ So you will no doubt see instantly that ...
❑ I'd now like to draw your attention to ...
❑ I think it's very significant that ...

– *getting attention for starting a presentation*

❑ So, ladies and gentlemen.
❑ OK. Can I have your attention, everyone?

- ❑ OK. Are we ready?
- ❑ All right, everyone!
- ❑ Let's start, shall we?
- ❑ Let's get underway, shall we?

AVOIDING

– *avoiding the question*

- ❑ I'm afraid I'm not in a position to comment on that.
- ❑ Well, it's rather difficult to say at present.
- ❑ I'm afraid I don't have enough information at my disposal to answer that.

– *playing for time*

- ❑ That's a very interesting question.
- ❑ That's a difficult question to answer.
- ❑ I'm glad you asked that question.
- ❑ You have raised an important point there.
- ❑ I'm sure you will appreciate how complicated this matter is.

B

BALANCING

– *balancing statements*

- ❑ On the one hand ..., but on the other ...
- ❑ Although ..., we mustn't forget ...
- ❑ In spite of ... / Despite ... I still think ...

C

CERTAINTY

– *expressing certainty*

- ❑ Yes. Definitely.

- ❑ Without a doubt.
- ❑ Absolutely. / Certainly.
- ❑ Oh, yes. I'm absolutely sure ...
- ❑ I'm quite sure ...
- ❑ I'm certain ...
- ❑ I'm positive it will ...
- ❑ No, I'm absolutely sure ... (it isn't) ...
- ❑ No, I'm quite sure ... (it isn't) ...
- ❑ No, definitely not.
- ❑ Certainly not. / Absolutely not.

CHALLENGING

– *challenging a point of view*

- ❑ I wonder if that view is justified in the light of ...
- ❑ I don't think you fully appreciate the fact that ...
- ❑ It would be in your own interest to consider the matter in view of ...
- ❑ If I were you, I would be inclined to consider the matter in view of ...

CHANGES

– *informing someone about changes in schedule*

- ❑ The original schedule has been updated.
- ❑ There is a slight change in the schedule.
- ❑ Before we begin, I would like to announce that ..., which means there's a slight change in the schedule.
- ❑ The ... has been postponed until ...
- ❑ I think we must postpone ... until ...
- ❑ Mr / Ms ...'s presentation has been moved to ...

- ❑ The room assignments have been changed.
- ❑ ..., scheduled to be held in ..., will now be meeting in ...
- ❑ Due to technical reasons ... the ... has been cancelled.
- ❑ Due to unforeseen circumstances ...
- ❑ Due to circumstances beyond our control ...
- ❑ Apologies from Mr / Ms ... Unfortunately he / she won't be able to participate.

– *making changes in travel arrangements*

- ❑ I'd like to make a change in my reservation.
- ❑ I'd like to change my ...
- ❑ Is it possible to exchange this ticket for ...?
- ❑ I'd like to cancel ...

CHECKING

– *asking someone to check information*

- ❑ Excuse me. Would you please check that ...?
- ❑ Is it possible for you to find out whether (or not) ...?
- ❑ I'd like to make sure that ...
- ❑ I'd just like to make sure that you've received ...

– *checking information*

- ❑ Just a moment, please. I'll have a look on the computer.
- ❑ I'm sorry. We have no record of your order.
- ❑ I'll have to check if we have a record of it.
- ❑ I'm sorry but we have no trace of it.
- ❑ Sorry, you don't appear on our ...
- ❑ Just a moment. I'll look up the details.
- ❑ I'll track this information down for you.

- ❑ I think we'd better get back to you on this one.

CLARIFICATION

– *asking for clarification and further explanation*

- ❑ Excuse me, could you explain how ... is done?
- ❑ Excuse me, could you review ...?
- ❑ Could / Would you, please, explain this process?
- ❑ Would you mind briefly going over ...?
- ❑ I wonder if you could ...
- ❑ Just to make sure I've got it right ...
- ❑ Did I understand you correctly that ...?
- ❑ To go back to what you were saying about ...
- ❑ Sorry to interrupt, but I wonder if you could / would explain about ... again for me.
- ❑ Sorry to interrupt, but I didn't quite catch what you said about ...
- ❑ While you're on the topic of ... may I ask ...?

CLOSING

– *ending a telephone conversation*

- ❑ Look forward to hearing from you then.
- ❑ I'm looking forward to meeting you.
- ❑ Thanks for calling. It's been nice talking to you.
- ❑ Nice talking to you, too.
- ❑ Fine. Hope to see you on ...
- ❑ Thank you, see you then. Goodbye.
- ❑ If I don't hear from you ... I'll give you a call ...

- ❑ That's just about it for now. I'll get back to you later.

– *closing a formal meeting*

- ❑ Is there any other business?
- ❑ Any further points?
- ❑ Is there anything else to discuss?
- ❑ I declare this meeting closed.
- ❑ If nobody has any further business, I think we can conclude the meeting for today.

– *rounding up (an informal meeting)*

- ❑ That just about wraps it up, I think.
- ❑ Well, I think that covers everything.
- ❑ I think that's all we have time for.
- ❑ Can we leave it at that, for now?
- ❑ Let's finish it here, everyone.
- ❑ Let's call it a day, shall we?
- ❑ If there's nothing else, I suggest we finish.
- ❑ Perhaps we can finish by ...
- ❑ That's all for today. Thank you.

– *concluding (negotiations)*

- ❑ Let me conclude by saying ...
- ❑ I'd like to conclude by stating that ...
- ❑ Allow me to conclude by highlighting the fact that ...
- ❑ In conclusion, I would like to reiterate ...
- ❑ I would now like to conclude my comments by assuring you that we are fully aware of the fact that ...

– *ending a presentation*

- ❑ Let me end by saying that ...
- ❑ I'd like to finish by ...
- ❑ I think I've spoken long enough now, so ...
- ❑ Well, that's it (really).

- ❑ Well, that completes my end of things.
- ❑ So, to sum up, ... Thank you for your attention, ...
- ❑ It's been a pleasure to ...
- ❑ I hope you enjoyed ... / found it ...
- ❑ If you have any questions I'll do my best to answer them.

COMPLAINTS

– *making polite complaints*

- ❑ I don't like to complain but ...
- ❑ I'm sorry to complain but ...
- ❑ Excuse me but I really feel I have to complain ...
- ❑ Excuse me a moment. I'm afraid ...
- ❑ To whom can I make a complaint?
- ❑ I've got a problem with ...
- ❑ Excuse me, the ... doesn't work properly.
- ❑ I'd like to return this ...
- ❑ Could you possibly change my room?

– *complaints in a restaurant*

- ❑ Excuse me, will it be much longer before we're served?
- ❑ Do you think we could change tables, please?
- ❑ Excuse me, this is not what I ordered.
- ❑ Excuse me, there's some mistake. This is not my order.
- ❑ Sorry to bother you but this ... is too ...

COMPROMISE

– *offering a compromise*

- ❑ Is that acceptable as a compromise solution?

- We're prepared to ... provided ...
- I think we could ... on condition that ...
- We're ready to ... on the understanding that ...
- We're more than ready to ... as long as ...

– *accepting a compromise*

- Yes. I think that would be perfectly acceptable.
- We would have no objections to that.
- That seems to be a reasonable compromise.
- To meet you halfway on this, I think we could agree to your condition.

– *rejecting a compromise*

- I'm sorry I can't go along with that.
- No, I'm afraid it won't work.
- No, I'm afraid I still couldn't agree.
- I'm afraid it just wouldn't be feasible.
- We find your offer unacceptable.
- You leave us little alternative but to turn ... down.

CONFIRMATION

– *confirming time and place*

- Just to confirm ...
- So, we're meeting in ... on ... at ...
- Right, so it's ...
- Ten o'clock it is then.
- When you get here, all you have to do is ...

– *confirming arrangements*

- I'm phoning about ...
- I'd just like to make sure you've received our ...

- ❑ I just wanted to make sure everything's in order.
- ❑ You haven't made it clear to us ...

– *asking for confirmation*

- ❑ Would I be correct in saying that ...?
- ❑ If I've understood correctly, you're saying that ...
- ❑ Am I correct in assuming that ...?
- ❑ Are you saying that ...?
- ❑ Basically, what you're saying is ...
- ❑ If you could, please confirm ...
- ❑ Could you send us confirmation by fax, please?

CONSENSUS

– *consensus*

- ❑ It would seem we have a consensus.
- ❑ Can I take it everyone's in favour?
- ❑ Are we all agreed on that?
- ❑ Well, it looks as if we're basically in agreement on this.

CONTACTING

– *asking to speak to someone on the telephone*

- ❑ Can I speak to ..., please?
- ❑ Could I talk to ..., please?
- ❑ I'm trying to get hold of ...
- ❑ I'm trying to contact ... / to get in touch with ...
- ❑ Would / Could you put me through to ..., please?

– *making an appointment*

- ❑ I'd like to make an appointment with ...
- ❑ Would it be possible to make an appointment with ...?
- ❑ I was wondering if it would be possible to make an appointment with ...

– *contacting the appropriate person and informing the visitor*

- ❑ Just one moment, please. I'll give him a call. / I'll page him.
- ❑ Would you like to take a seat?
- ❑ He's expecting you.
- ❑ He'll be with you in a moment.
- ❑ I'm sorry. He's just stepped out for a while.
- ❑ He'll be right back.
- ❑ I'm sorry. He's not answering at the moment.
- ❑ I'll try again in a moment.
- ❑ I'm very sorry, but Mr / Ms ... is not here at the moment.
- ❑ Perhaps there's someone else who can help.

– *approaching others*

- ❑ Mr ... / Ms ...?
- ❑ It's ..., isn't it?
- ❑ Excuse me, are you ...?
- ❑ Hello, you must be ...

– *referring to future contacts*

- ❑ Well, if there's anything else you would like to know about, why not give me a call later?
- ❑ We'll be delighted to give you all the assistance we can.
- ❑ We'll send you the info / brochures / price lists later.

- ❑ Well, look, if ever you're in ..., why don't you drop in and see us? I'd be delighted to show you around.
- ❑ I'm certain something will come (out) of this.

CORRECTING

– *correcting misunderstandings*

- ❑ I'm afraid there seems to have been a slight misunderstanding.
- ❑ We seem to be talking at cross purposes.
- ❑ I think you've misunderstood me / us.
- ❑ I'm afraid I haven't made myself clear enough.
- ❑ That isn't quite what I said.
- ❑ With all due respect, that's not what I said.

D

DECLINING, see also REJECTING

– *declining invitations*

- ❑ I'd love to but ...
- ❑ I'm awfully sorry but ...
- ❑ I'm afraid I can't ...
- ❑ It's really nice of you to ask, but ...
- ❑ Well, I hope you don't mind, but ...
- ❑ I'd really like to but I'm afraid I can't.
- ❑ Sorry, no. We can't make it tonight. Maybe some other time.
- ❑ Sorry, no. I've already arranged to go somewhere else.

– *responding to an invitation that has been declined*

- ❑ All right. Never mind.
- ❑ Some other time then.
- ❑ Oh dear. Well, I quite understand, of course.

DIGRESSING

– *digressing during a presentation*

- ❑ I'd just like to mention in passing that ...
- ❑ Please allow me to digress for a while.
- ❑ If you'll let me, I'd like to digress for a while.

- ❑ Let me get back to my main point.
- ❑ To return to my original ...
- ❑ But that's really a side issue. Let me return to what I was saying about ...

DIRECTIONS

– *asking for directions*

- ❑ I'm looking for the ...
- ❑ How far is it to ... from here?
- ❑ Excuse me, is it a long way to ...?
- ❑ Excuse me, can you tell me the way to ..., please?
- ❑ Excuse me, can you tell me where ... is, please?
- ❑ Excuse me, could you tell me how to get to ..., please?
- ❑ Can you tell me where the .... is taking place?

– *giving simple directions*

- ❑ Walk / Go down / along this street ...

- ❑ Walk straight on / ahead.
- ❑ Go straight on until you come to ... / as far as ...
- ❑ Turn right / left at ...
- ❑ Take the first turning right / left.
- ❑ It's not very far. / It's quite near here.
- ❑ It won't take you long.
- ❑ It's about ... minutes from here.
- ❑ It'll take you about ... minutes to get there.

– *giving directions on the premises*

- ❑ Straight ahead, past the lifts / elevators, on your right.
- ❑ Take the first turning on the left.
- ❑ It's at the end of the corridor.
- ❑ Take the lift / elevator to the fifth floor.
- ❑ If you'd like to come with me I'll take you there.
- ❑ I'll get someone to show you the way.
- ❑ I'll try and get someone to help you.

DISAGREEING

– *expressing strong disagreement*

- ❑ (I'm sorry, but) I totally disagree with you.
- ❑ (I'm sorry, but) I don't agree with you.
- ❑ (I'm sorry, but) I don't agree at all.
- ❑ (I'm sorry, but) I disagree entirely.
- ❑ Well, I (really) can't agree with you on that.
- ❑ You're completely mistaken ...
- ❑ Under no circumstances could I agree to that.
- ❑ What you're saying is just not feasible.
- ❑ No way.
- ❑ I can't accept your point of view.
- ❑ I'm sorry but that's really out of the question.

- ❑ To be quite frank, ...
- ❑ To put it bluntly, ...
- ❑ With respect, ...

– *expressing neutral disagreement*

- ❑ I feel I must disagree.
- ❑ I can't say I share your view.
- ❑ I respect your opinion, of course; however ...
- ❑ I'm not totally convinced by your argument.
- ❑ We'll have to agree to differ.
- ❑ Do you really think so?
- ❑ Well, I can't help feeling that ...
- ❑ Well, personally I think that ...
- ❑ I don't know about that.
- ❑ I wouldn't say that.
- ❑ I'm not so sure I agree with you.
- ❑ Well, I can't say I'm completely happy with the idea.

DISCUSSION

– *guiding the discussion (in a meeting)*

- ❑ Could we keep / stick to the agenda, please?
- ❑ This isn't relevant to our discussion.
- ❑ We seem to be losing sight of the main point.
- ❑ The question is ...
- ❑ What we're trying to do is ...

– *keeping order (in a meeting)*

- ❑ Order! Order!
- ❑ We can't all speak at the same time.
- ❑ Could we stick to the agenda, please?
- ❑ Mr / Ms..., would you mind addressing your remarks to the Chair?

– *moving on to a new point (in a meeting)*

- ❑ Could we move on to item four on the agenda?
- ❑ Can we now go to ...?
- ❑ Now I'd like to turn to ...
- ❑ Has anyone anything further they would wish to add?

DOUBT

– *expressing doubt*

- ❑ Possibly. / Perhaps. / Maybe.
- ❑ I doubt it.
- ❑ I have my doubts.
- ❑ It's doubtful.
- ❑ It's highly unlikely.
- ❑ Well, you never know, of course.
- ❑ No one can say for sure.
- ❑ I wouldn't like to say for sure.
- ❑ I'm not really sure.

DRINKS

– *offering drinks*

- ❑ Would you like a drink?
- ❑ What would you like to drink?
- ❑ Drink, anyone?
- ❑ Can I get you a drink?
- ❑ What are you having?

– *accepting drinks*

- ❑ I'd love one.
- ❑ Thank you. I'll have a ...
- ❑ Thank you very much. I'll have a ..., please.
- ❑ Thank you. What do you recommend?

– *refusing drinks*

- ❑ Not for me, thank you.
- ❑ No more for me, thanks.
- ❑ Not just yet. Maybe later.
- ❑ No, thanks. I'm driving.
- ❑ No, thank you. I don't drink.

E

EATING

– *informing people about the meal*

- ❑ Dinner will be ready in a minute.
- ❑ I think we're ready to begin serving dinner.
- ❑ Sorry to interrupt, but dinner is ready / served.

– *getting a table at a restaurant*

- ❑ A table for two, please.
- ❑ Good evening. We'd like a table for three, please.
- ❑ Good evening. We have a table reservation.

- ❑ Yes, sir / madam. What name, please?
- ❑ Just one moment, please.
- ❑ This way, please.
- ❑ Certainly sir / madam. Would you care / like to follow me, please?

– *deciding on food in a restaurant*

- ❑ What about number four?
- ❑ What would you like?
- ❑ What shall we have to start with / to follow / to finish with?
- ❑ Well, the ... sounds delicious, doesn't it?
- ❑ That sounds very nice.

- ❑ Can you tell me what ... is?
- ❑ Have you made your selection?
- ❑ Have you decided?
- ❑ Are you ready to order?
- ❑ What do you recommend?
- ❑ I'll have ... / I'd like ...

– *addressing the waiter*

- ❑ Can I have / see the menu, please?
- ❑ I wonder if you could help us.
- ❑ We're ready to order.
- ❑ Could I have the bill, please?

– *table talk*

- ❑ Could you pass me the ..., please?
- ❑ Can I pass you the ...?
- ❑ Would you like some (more) ...?

EMPHASIZING

– *expressing emphatic views*

- ❑ I particularly want to emphasize the fact that ...
- ❑ It is essential that ...
- ❑ I feel this is a vital issue.
- ❑ I consider this point to be of the utmost importance.

ENDING (see CLOSING)

EXAMPLES

– *giving examples*

- ❑ Let me give you an example.
- ❑ One example might be ...
- ❑ To illustrate this point ...

EXCUSES

– *excusing oneself*

- ❑ Excuse me a moment.
- ❑ I'm afraid I must leave you for a minute.
- ❑ I'll be right back.

EXPLAINING

– *asking for clarification and further explanation*

- ❑ Excuse me, could you explain how ... is done?
- ❑ Excuse me, could you review ...?
- ❑ Could / Would you, please, explain this process?
- ❑ Would you mind briefly going over ...?
- ❑ I wonder if you could ...
- ❑ Just to make sure I've got it right, ...
- ❑ Did I understand you correctly that ...?
- ❑ To go back to what you were saying about ...
- ❑ Sorry to interrupt, but I wonder if you could / would explain about ... again for me.
- ❑ Sorry to interrupt, but I didn't quite catch what you said about ...
- ❑ While you're on the topic of ... may I ask ...?

– *explaining the purpose of a presentation*

- ❑ I'd like to talk about ...
- ❑ I shall be dealing with ...
- ❑ I'm here to tell you (all) about ...
- ❑ I'm here to present ...
- ❑ My purpose today is to talk about ...
- ❑ I'd like to just give you a brief breakdown of ...

- To start with ..., then ...
- Firstly, ... and secondly, ... and finally ...

– *stating the purpose of a meeting*
- Before we begin I'd like to make a few remarks concerning ...
- The most important points seem to be ...
- Let me start by giving you an outline of my proposals ...
- Our purpose in meeting here today is to ...
- What we have to do this morning is ...
- By the end of this meeting we must have decided ...

F

FINISHING (see also CLOSING)

– *finishing a point*
- OK. So much for ...
- That's all I'm going to say about ...
- And that's all I have to say about ...
- So that's ...
- OK. So we've looked at ...

FLOOR

– *giving someone the floor*
- Mr / Ms ..., would you like to say something about this?
- At this point I'd like to give the floor to ...
- Mr ..., I think you know something about this. Perhaps I can bring you in here.
- Have you got anything to say about this, ...?
- Very well ... The floor is yours...
- The floor is open.

– *taking the floor*
- ❑ Mr Chairman, could I have the floor, please?
- ❑ Excuse me, Madam Chairman, may I say something, please?
- ❑ With the Chair's permission, I'd like to take up the point about ...

FOOD (see EATING)

G

GENERALIZING

– *generalizing*
- ❑ But on the whole ...
- ❑ In general, ... / Generally speaking, ...
- ❑ All in all, ...
- ❑ All things considered, ...

GOODBYE

– *saying goodbye to an acquaintance*
- ❑ Be seeing you. / So long.
- ❑ OK, see you then. / See you later.
- ❑ Sure. See you then.

– *saying goodbye formally*
- ❑ Well, I hope we meet again in the very near future.
- ❑ I look forward to hearing from you soon.
- ❑ I look forward to seeing you in / at ...
- ❑ I look forward to receiving your offer / price list.
- ❑ Nice talking to you. Thank you so much.

– *ending a telephone conversation*
- ❑ Look forward to hearing from you then.

- ❑ I'm looking forward to meeting you.
- ❑ Thanks for calling. It's been nice talking to you.
- ❑ Nice talking to you too.
- ❑ Fine. Hope to see you on ...
- ❑ Thank you, see you then. Goodbye.
- ❑ If I don't hear from you ... I'll give you a call ...
- ❑ That's just about it for now. I'll get back to you later.

GRANTING

– *granting permission*

- ❑ Sure. / Certainly. / Yes, of course.
- ❑ Of course you can / may.
- ❑ Yes, by all means.
- ❑ Please do.
- ❑ Go ahead.

– *agreeing on meeting later*

- ❑ All right. What time and where?
- ❑ Shall we say at seven in the lobby?
- ❑ Yes, I don't see why not.
- ❑ OK, seven it is then. See you later.

GREETING

– *greeting people for the first time*

- ❑ Pleased to meet you. I'm ... from ...
- ❑ I'm ... Pleased to meet you.
- ❑ How do you do?
- ❑ Nice to meet you.
- ❑ Glad to meet you too.
- ❑ Kind of you to come and meet me.
- ❑ I've been looking forward to meeting you.

– *greeting an acquaintance*

- ❑ Hello, ... Good to see you again.
- ❑ Nice to see you again.
- ❑ Hello, ... How are you?
- ❑ Hi. How's it going?
- ❑ How are you keeping?
- ❑ How are things with you?
- ❑ What have you been up to since the last time we met?
- ❑ Oh, not so bad, you know. You?
- ❑ Well, I'm still alive.
- ❑ No complaints.
- ❑ Very well, thank you. How about you?
- ❑ Hi, ... Pretty good, thanks. And you?
- ❑ All right. It's been some time. Nearly ...
- ❑ Really. Has it been that long?
- ❑ I'm so sorry, I can't quite remember your name.

– *asking about someone*

- ❑ How's ...? / How are ...?
- ❑ Have you heard from ... lately?

GROUP WORK

– *starting group work*

- ❑ I suppose we'd better start by introducing ourselves.
- ❑ I think we should begin by ...
- ❑ This group is going to deal with ...
- ❑ We have to give a short report on ...
- ❑ Would anyone like to volunteer to serve as spokesperson?
- ❑ Would anyone like to volunteer to take the minutes?
- ❑ Who would like to take notes?

- ❑ Would anyone here like to represent this group?
- ❑ Who would like to report our conclusions?

– *presenting group work*

- ❑ Our task was to ...
- ❑ The objective of our group was ...
- ❑ From the outset, our group ...
- ❑ The discussion then focused on ...
- ❑ This led to ...
- ❑ It was agreed that ...
- ❑ A number of points emerged from our discussion.
- ❑ We also stressed the ...
- ❑ We would like to underline the following points.
- ❑ This led us to make the following proposals.
- ❑ Lastly, the discussion turned to ...
- ❑ All in all, ...
- ❑ As far as our group is concerned, ...

GUESTS

– *welcoming visitors to your workplace*

- ❑ Glad you could join us today.
- ❑ We're very pleased to have you with us today.
- ❑ On behalf of ... I would like to welcome you all here today to ...

– *inviting people*

- ❑ Would you like to ...?
- ❑ Would you care to ...?
- ❑ I was wondering if you would like to ...
- ❑ I was wondering if you would care to come to ...

- ❑ I was wondering if you would like to join me for ...
- ❑ How about going ...?
- ❑ Do you feel like spending the evening ...?

– *making guests feel welcome*

- ❑ Hello. How are you?
- ❑ Glad you could make it.
- ❑ I'm so pleased you could come.
- ❑ Please come in and make yourself at home.
- ❑ Here, let me take your coat.
- ❑ May I take your coat?

– *asking about someone*

- ❑ How's ... / How are ...?
- ❑ Have you heard from ... lately?

H

HESITATION

– *expressing positive hesitation*

- ❑ Um ... well, actually ...
- ❑ How shall I put it?
- ❑ Well, in fact ... you see ...

HOTELS

– *asking about hotel accommodation*

- ❑ Do you have any vacancies?
- ❑ I'd like to inquire about ...
- ❑ I'd like to make a reservation for ...
- ❑ I'd like to know the price of ...
- ❑ How much do you charge for a single / double room?
- ❑ Is breakfast included in the price?
- ❑ What credit cards do you take?

– *dealing with hotel reservations*

- ❑ A single or a double room?
- ❑ A single / double room costs ...
- ❑ When will you be arriving?
- ❑ And how many nights is it?
- ❑ How long will you be staying?
- ❑ What dates did you have in mind?
- ❑ How will you be paying?
- ❑ Thank you for your reservation.
- ❑ How will you be confirming your reservation?
- ❑ Will you send me the names by fax?
- ❑ We'll give you two weeks to confirm. OK?
- ❑ Could you give me your credit card number, please?

I

IDENTIFICATION

– *asking for identification on the telephone*

- ❑ Who's calling, please?
- ❑ Who shall I say is calling?
- ❑ Yes, certainly. Could I have your name, please?
- ❑ Could I have your name again, please?
- ❑ Would you spell that for me, please?
- ❑ I wonder if you would mind spelling that for me, please.

– *finding out someone's identity*

- ❑ Who shall I say is here?
- ❑ Can / May I have your name, please?
- ❑ What company are you from?
- ❑ Do you have an appointment?

- ❑ Who do you have an appointment with?
- ❑ Excuse me but I didn't quite catch your name.
- ❑ Excuse me, what was your name, again?
- ❑ I'm sorry, what company did you say you worked for / represented?
- ❑ If you'd just give me your name and address, I'll make sure you get all the information you want as soon as possible.
- ❑ If I could just have your name in the visitors' book?

IGNORANCE

– *expressing ignorance*

- ❑ I really wouldn't like to say.
- ❑ I must admit I don't know.
- ❑ I've really no idea.
- ❑ I really couldn't say.
- ❑ I haven't a clue.
- ❑ I don't have the slightest idea.

IMPROBABILITY

– *expressing improbability*

- ❑ I don't think so.
- ❑ Probably not.
- ❑ No, I'm sure it wouldn't.
- ❑ The chances are it wouldn't.
- ❑ It's highly unlikely.
- ❑ There's very little chance of that happening.

INFORMATION

– *adding information*

- ❑ There are certain points you should bear in mind.

- ❑ If we look at it in another light ...
- ❑ There are other considerations ...
- ❑ I wonder if you've considered ...
- ❑ Seen from another angle, one could ...
- ❑ Let me elaborate ...
- ❑ I'll explain it in greater detail.

– *asking for further information*

- ❑ Could you be a little more precise?
- ❑ Could you give us some details about ...?
- ❑ Could you expand on that?
- ❑ I'm sorry but could you explain in a little more detail?
- ❑ Would you care to elaborate on that?

– *asking someone to check information*

- ❑ Excuse me. Would you please check that ...?
- ❑ Is it possible for you to find out whether (or not) ... ?
- ❑ I'd like to make sure that ...
- ❑ I'd just like to make sure that you've received ...

– *checking information*

- ❑ Just a moment, please. I'll have a look on the computer.
- ❑ I'm sorry. We have no record of your order.
- ❑ I'll have to check if we have a record of it.
- ❑ I'm sorry but we have no trace of it.
- ❑ Sorry, you don't appear on our ...
- ❑ Just a moment. I'll look up the details.
- ❑ I'll track this information down for you.
- ❑ I think we'd better get back to you on this one.

INFORMING

– *informing reception of your arrival*

- ❑ I have an appointment with Mr / Ms ... at ...
- ❑ I'm here from ...
- ❑ My name is ... I'm here to see ...
- ❑ I'm ... Can you tell me where ... is, please?

– *contacting the appropriate person and informing the visitor*

- ❑ Just one moment, please. I'll give him a call. / I'll page him.
- ❑ Would you like to take a seat?
- ❑ He's expecting you.
- ❑ He'll be with you in a moment.
- ❑ I'm sorry. He's just stepped out for a while.
- ❑ He'll be right back.
- ❑ I'm sorry. He's not answering at the moment.
- ❑ I'll try again in a moment.
- ❑ I'm very sorry, but Mr / Ms ... is not here at the moment.
- ❑ Perhaps there's someone else who can help.

– *paging*

- ❑ Paging Mr / Ms ...
- ❑ Will Mr / Ms ..., please report to the ...?
- ❑ Will Mr / Ms ... kindly go to the ...?
- ❑ Oh, I'm just being paged. / I've just been paged.

– *informing people about the meal*

- ❑ Dinner will be ready in a minute.
- ❑ I think we're ready to begin serving dinner.
- ❑ Sorry to interrupt, but dinner is ready / served.

– *informing someone about changes in schedule*

- ❑ The original schedule has been updated.
- ❑ There is a slight change in the schedule.
- ❑ Before we begin, I would like to announce that ..., which means there's a slight change in the schedule.
- ❑ The ... has been postponed until ...
- ❑ I think we must postpone ... until ...
- ❑ Mr / Ms ...'s presentation has been moved to ...
- ❑ The room assignments have been changed.
- ❑ ..., scheduled to be held in ..., will now be meeting in ...
- ❑ Due to technical reasons ... the ... has been cancelled.
- ❑ Due to unforeseen circumstances ...
- ❑ Due to circumstances beyond our control...
- ❑ Apologies from Mr / Ms ... Unfortunately he / she won't be able to participate.

INQUIRING (see also QUESTIONS)

– *inquiring about arrangements*

- ❑ I'd just like to know whether it's possible to ...
- ❑ Where do I sign up for ...?
- ❑ Where can I get ...?
- ❑ Who do I see to arrange ...?
- ❑ To whom do I talk to arrange ...?
- ❑ I need ... How can that be arranged?
- ❑ How can I get hold of ...?
- ❑ Where's ... being held?
- ❑ Can you tell me where ... is, please?

– *inquiring about problems*

- ❑ I was told that you could possibly / perhaps help me.
- ❑ Do you have any idea where I can ...?
- ❑ Could you help me find ... please?
- ❑ Excuse me. I sent a package of ... to this address ...

INTRODUCING

– *introducing a point*

- ❑ I'd like to bring up the point about ...
- ❑ I'd like to bring up the question of ...
- ❑ I'd like to mention briefly ...
- ❑ At this point ...

– *starting another point*

- ❑ Now I'd like to talk about ...
- ❑ Now I want to say a few words about ...
- ❑ Now I'd like to move on to ...
- ❑ Now I'd like to proceed by ...
- ❑ As you see, I now want to ...
- ❑ If I may, I'd now like to draw your attention to ...
- ❑ Next I'd like to concentrate on ...
- ❑ The next point I wish to deal with ....

INTRODUCTIONS

– *introducing yourself on the telephone*

- ❑ Hello. This is ... phoning from ...
- ❑ This is ... I'm calling from ...
- ❑ My name is ...
- ❑ Good morning / afternoon / evening. This is ... from ...

– *introducing yourself*

- ❑ Let me introduce myself. I'm ...
- ❑ Oh, I'm sorry. I haven't introduced myself. I'm ...

– *introducing others*

- ❑ Can / May I introduce you to my colleague, Mr / Ms ...?
- ❑ ... , I'd like you to meet ... He / She works for ...
- ❑ Mr / Ms ..., please allow me to introduce you to ...
- ❑ ..., this is ... He's our ...
- ❑ I don't believe you two have met before, have you?
- ❑ This is ... from ... John Smith, our ...
- ❑ I'd like you all to meet my friend ...

– *introducing yourself and your workplace*

- ❑ My name is ... I'm ...
- ❑ As you know our job here mainly concerns ...
- ❑ I'm in charge of ...
- ❑ Here at ... we ...
- ❑ I'd like to show you the way we do things around here.

– *introducing the speaker (at a conference)*

- ❑ It's my pleasure to introduce our first speaker ..., who will be talking about ...
- ❑ Our next speaker is ..., who will speak about ...
- ❑ The title of our next talk is ..., given by ... from ...

INVITATIONS

– *inviting people*

- ❑ Would you like to ...?
- ❑ Would you care to ..?
- ❑ I was wondering if you would like to ...
- ❑ I was wondering if you would care to come to ...
- ❑ I was wondering if you would like to join me for ...
- ❑ How about going ...?
- ❑ Do you feel like spending the evening ...?

– *accepting invitations*

- ❑ I'd love to.
- ❑ I'd be delighted to.
- ❑ That would be very nice.
- ❑ Sounds like a great idea.
- ❑ Yes. I'd like to very much. Thanks.
- ❑ That's very kind of you. I'd like that very much.

– *declining invitations*

- ❑ I'd love to but ...
- ❑ I'm awfully sorry but ...
- ❑ I'm afraid I can't.
- ❑ It's really nice of you to ask, but ...
- ❑ Well, I hope you don't mind but ...
- ❑ I'd really like to but I'm afraid I can't.
- ❑ Sorry, no. We can't make it tonight. Maybe some other time.
- ❑ Sorry, no. I've already arranged to go somewhere else.

– *responding to an invitation that has been declined*

- ❑ All right. Never mind.

- ❑ Some other time then.
- ❑ Oh dear. Well, I quite understand, of course.

K

KEEPING ORDER

– *keeping order (in a meeting)*

- ❑ Order! Order!
- ❑ We can't all speak at the same time.
- ❑ Could we stick to the agenda, please?
- ❑ Mr / Ms ... Would you care to address your remarks to the Chair?

L

LEAVING

– *taking your leave*

- ❑ I really should be going now.
- ❑ Well, I'm afraid I have to be going now.
- ❑ Well, it's been marvellous running into you like this.
- ❑ Nice seeing you, too.
- ❑ I really must be off now.
- ❑ I'd better be going, too.
- ❑ Well, I really can't be staying any longer.
- ❑ Well, I'd better be going, I suppose.
- ❑ Well, it really is time I was off.
- ❑ Well, I think it's about time I started making my way home.
- ❑ Well, I really must be getting along.
- ❑ Well, I think I had better think about leaving.

– *saying goodbye to an acquaintance*
- ❑ Be seeing you. / So long.
- ❑ OK, see you then. / See you later.
- ❑ Sure. See you then.

– *saying goodbye formally*
- ❑ Well, I hope we (shall) meet again in the very near future.
- ❑ I look forward to hearing from you soon.
- ❑ I look forward to seeing you in / at ...
- ❑ I look forward to receiving your offer / price list.
- ❑ Nice talking to you. Thank you so much.

– *excusing oneself*
- ❑ Excuse me a moment.
- ❑ I'm afraid I must leave you for a minute.
- ❑ I'll be right back.

M

MEETINGS (see PARTS 4, page 139, and 5, page 144, in LIST 2)

MESSAGES

– *asking about messages*
- ❑ My name's ... Do you have any messages for me?
- ❑ I'm expecting a message ...
- ❑ Were there any messages for me today?

– *leaving messages*
- ❑ I'd like to leave a message ...
- ❑ I'm expecting a phone call from ... If he phones could you ...?

❑ If anyone phones for me, would you please tell them ...

– *giving messages*

❑ There's a message for you.
❑ A Ms ... was asking for you. She said she would try and get hold of you later.
❑ She said that she would phone back later.
❑ She couldn't wait for you any longer, but she did leave a message ...

MINUTES

– *dealing with the minutes*

❑ May I read the minutes?
❑ I'll read the minutes of the last meeting.
❑ It was decided that ...
❑ Would someone move that the minutes of the last meeting be accepted?
❑ We can take the minutes as read.

MOTIONS

– *motioning*

❑ I propose that ...
❑ I would like to propose the motion that ...
❑ I would like to move that ...
❑ With the Chair's / Chairman's permission, I move that ...

– *seconding a motion*

❑ Would anyone like to second the motion?
❑ Anyone wish to second that motion?
❑ Seconded! / I'll second that motion.
❑ Seconded by Mr / Ms ...

– *the language of voting*

- ❑ Can I have a show of hands?
- ❑ Those *for* the motion, please?
- ❑ Will those in favour of the motion raise their right hands?
- ❑ Those against?
- ❑ Any abstentions?
- ❑ The motion is carried unanimously.
- ❑ The motion has been carried by six votes to five.
- ❑ The motion has been rejected / defeated by six votes to five.

N

NEGOTIATIONS (see PART 7 in LIST 2, page 154)

NEWS

– *breaking good news*

- ❑ Good news, everyone!
- ❑ Guess what ...?
- ❑ Did you know that ...?
- ❑ Have you heard that ...?

– *responding to good news*

- ❑ Really?
- ❑ That's great news!
- ❑ Congratulations!
- ❑ That's great!
- ❑ You must be very pleased.
- ❑ Good. Glad to hear it.

– *breaking bad news*

- ❑ Bad news, I'm afraid.
- ❑ I've got some bad news for you, I'm afraid.

– *responding to bad news*

❑ I'm very sorry to hear that.

❑ That *is* bad news.

❑ What a pity.

❑ That's a shame.

O

OFFERING

– *offering drinks*

❑ Would you like a drink?

❑ What would you like to drink?

❑ Drink, anyone?

❑ Can I get you a drink?

❑ What are you having?

– *offering assistance*

❑ Can I help you in some way?

❑ May I be of assistance?

❑ Would you like me to do it for you?

❑ Can I give you a hand?

– *offering a compromise*

❑ Is that acceptable as a compromise solution?

❑ We're prepared to ... provided ...

❑ I think we could ... on condition that ...

❑ We're ready to ... on the understanding that ...

❑ We're more than ready to ... as long as ...

OPENING

– *opening a conference*

❑ It's my pleasure to welcome you all to this conference.

- It's my honour as the chairperson to declare this ... open.
- It's my privilege to chair this session.

– *opening a formal meeting*

- Ladies and gentlemen, I declare the meeting open.
- Let's get down to business, everyone, shall we?
- Let's get this meeting underway.
- Well, I think we all know why we're here.

– *opening an informal meeting*

- Let's get started, shall we?
- Let's get down to business, shall we?
- First of all ...
- To begin with ...
- Let me start by ...
- I'd like to start by ...

OPINIONS

– *asking for opinions*

- What do you think about / of ...?
- What's your opinion of ...?
- How do you feel about ...?
- How do you react to ...?
- What are your views on ...?
- I'd like to hear your views on ...

– *giving opinions*

- I think / feel that ...
- In my opinion ...
- As I see it, ...
- I (firmly) believe that ...
- It's my belief / opinion that ...
- From my point of view, ...

- ❑ As far as I am concerned, ...

– *giving tentative opinions*

- ❑ It seems to me that ...
- ❑ I would say that ...
- ❑ As far as I'm able to judge ...
- ❑ I think it would be fair to say that ...

– *expressing emphatic views*

- ❑ It is essential that ...
- ❑ I particularly want to emphasize the fact that ...
- ❑ I feel this is a vital issue.
- ❑ I consider this point to be of the utmost importance.

– *challenging a point of view*

- ❑ I don't think you fully appreciate the fact that ...
- ❑ I wonder if that view is justified in the light of ...
- ❑ It would be in your own interest to consider the matter in view of ...
- ❑ If I were you, I would be inclined to consider the matter in view of ...

P

PAGING

– *paging*

- ❑ Paging Mr / Ms ...
- ❑ Will Mr / Ms ..., please report to the ...?
- ❑ Will Mr / Ms ... kindly go to the ...?
- ❑ Oh, I'm just being paged. / I've just been paged.

PERMISSION

– *asking for permission*

- ❑ Excuse me, may / can / could I ...?
- ❑ Do you think I could ...?
- ❑ I wonder if I could ...
- ❑ Is it all right if I ...?
- ❑ Do you mind if I ...?

– *granting permission*

- ❑ Sure. / Certainly. / Yes, of course.
- ❑ Of course you can / may.
- ❑ Yes, by all means.
- ❑ Please do.
- ❑ Go ahead.

– *refusing permission*

- ❑ No, I'm sorry.
- ❑ I'm afraid you can't.
- ❑ I'm sorry but you can't.
- ❑ Well, I'd rather you didn't, if you don't mind.

PLACE

– *arranging place*

- ❑ Where should we meet?
- ❑ Let's meet at ...
- ❑ What about if we meet at ...? / What about meeting at ...?
- ❑ I suggest we meet at ... / Why don't we meet at ...?
- ❑ What's the address?
- ❑ Do you know the address?
- ❑ Do you know how to get here?
- ❑ Should I take a cab / taxi?
- ❑ Shall I pick you up at ...?

- ❑ Just to make sure I've got the time and place right ...

– *accepting time and place*

- ❑ Fine with me.
- ❑ OK. Let's meet there.
- ❑ Suits me fine.
- ❑ I'll be there.
- ❑ I'll be waiting for you in / at ...
- ❑ Good. What time would be most suitable for you?
- ❑ Great. I'll come and pick you up at your hotel at ...

– *rejecting time and place*

- ❑ Sorry. I'm already booked.
- ❑ Sorry. That won't work.
- ❑ No. I'm sorry. That's no good.
- ❑ I'm afraid I've got something else on.
- ❑ Wait a minute. No, sorry. I've got something else then.

– *confirming time and place*

- ❑ So, we're meeting in ... on ... at ...
- ❑ Right, so it's ...
- ❑ Ten o'clock it is then.
- ❑ Just to confirm ...
- ❑ When you get here, all you have to do is ...

POINTS

– *introducing a point*

- ❑ I'd like to bring up the point about ...
- ❑ I'd like to bring up the question of ...
- ❑ I'd like to mention briefly ...
- ❑ At this point ...

– *rephrasing a point*

- ❑ Perhaps I haven't made myself clear.
- ❑ Sorry. I'm probably not making myself clear.
- ❑ Let me put it another way.
- ❑ Allow me to rephrase that.
- ❑ To be more specific, ...
- ❑ Basically, what I'm trying to say is ...
- ❑ Perhaps I should make that clear by saying ...

– *playing down a point*

- ❑ OK. But this is a minor issue.
- ❑ Yes, but this is only of secondary importance.
- ❑ Perhaps. But this, after all, is a relatively small point.

– *drawing attention to a point*

- ❑ As you can see, ...
- ❑ As you have noticed, ...
- ❑ I think it's very significant that ...
- ❑ So you will no doubt see instantly that ...
- ❑ I'd now like to draw your attention to ...

– *finishing a point*

- ❑ OK. So much for ...
- ❑ That's all I'm going to say about ...
- ❑ And that's all I have to say about ...
- ❑ So that's ...
- ❑ OK. So we've looked at ...

– *moving on to a new point*

- ❑ Could we move on to item four on the agenda?
- ❑ Now I'd like to turn to ...
- ❑ Can we now go to ...?

- ❑ Has anyone anything further they would wish to add?

– *starting another point*

- ❑ Now I'd like to talk about ...
- ❑ Now I want to say a few words about ...
- ❑ Now I'd like to move on to ...
- ❑ Now I'd like to proceed by ...
- ❑ As you see, I now want to ...
- ❑ If I may, I'd now like to draw your attention to ...
- ❑ Next I'd like to concentrate on ...
- ❑ The next point I wish to deal with ...

POSTPONING

– *postponing (in a meeting)*

- ❑ If no one has any objections, I suggest we leave this matter until our next meeting.
- ❑ Well, ladies and gentlemen, with your approval, I propose to defer this matter until ...

– *leaving things open*

- ❑ Let's leave it like that.
- ❑ Let's leave it open for the time being.
- ❑ Let's decide later, shall we?
- ❑ OK. I'll get back to you later on that.

PREFERENCE

– *stating preferences*

- ❑ I'd rather ... than ...
- ❑ I'd rather not ...
- ❑ I prefer ... to ...

PRESENTING

– *getting attention for starting a presentation*

- ❑ OK. Are we ready?
- ❑ All right, everyone!
- ❑ Let's start, shall we?
- ❑ Let's get underway, shall we?
- ❑ So, ladies and gentlemen.
- ❑ OK. Can I have your attention, everyone?

– *starting a presentation*

- ❑ Good morning, ladies and gentlemen. Welcome to ...
- ❑ My name is ... and I'm a(n) ... with ...
- ❑ On behalf of ..., I'd like to welcome you all here to ...
- ❑ As you know, I'm here to present ... to you.
- ❑ Nice to see you all here.
- ❑ Let me begin by saying ...
- ❑ Let's start by looking at ...
- ❑ First I'd like to say a few words about ...

– *explaining the purpose of a presentation*

- ❑ I shall be dealing with ...
- ❑ I'm here to tell you (all) about ...
- ❑ I'd like to talk about ...
- ❑ I'm here to present ...
- ❑ My purpose today is to talk about ...
- ❑ I'd like to just give you a brief breakdown of ...
- ❑ To start with ..., then ...
- ❑ Firstly, ... and secondly, ... and finally ...

– *digressing during a presentation*

- ❑ I'd just like to mention in passing that ...

- ❑ Please allow me to digress for a while.
- ❑ If you let me, I'd like to digress for a while.

- ❑ Let me get back to my main point.
- ❑ To return to my original ...
- ❑ But that's really a side issue. Let me return to what I was saying about ...

– *ending a presentation*

- ❑ Let me end by saying that ...
- ❑ I'd like to finish by ...
- ❑ I think I've spoken long enough now, so ...
- ❑ Well, that's it (really).
- ❑ Well, that completes my end of things.
- ❑ So, to sum up, ... Thank you for your attention, ...
- ❑ It's been a pleasure to ...
- ❑ I hope you enjoyed ... / found it ...
- ❑ If you have any questions I'll do my best to answer them.

– *presenting group work*

- ❑ Our task was to ...
- ❑ The objective of our group was ...
- ❑ From the outset, our group ...
- ❑ The discussion then focused on ...
- ❑ This led to ...
- ❑ It was agreed that ...
- ❑ A number of points emerged from our discussion.
- ❑ We also stressed the ...
- ❑ We would like to underline the following points.
- ❑ This led us to make the following proposals.
- ❑ Lastly, the discussion turned to ...
- ❑ All in all, ...

- ❑ As far as our group is concerned, ...

– *asking presenters questions*

- ❑ I was wondering if I understood correctly ...
- ❑ Thank you for an interesting presentation. Referring to what you said about ...
- ❑ About what you said concerning ...
- ❑ I was wondering if I could ask something about ...

– *responding to questions from the audience*

- ❑ That's a good question.
- ❑ I'm glad you asked me that question.
- ❑ I thought someone would ask me about that.
- ❑ I'll have to give some thought to that.
- ❑ I'm not sure if I understood your question.
- ❑ I'm afraid I'm unable to answer your question.
- ❑ If I understood you correctly, ...
- ❑ Maybe it would be better if we had a word afterwards.

PROBABILITY

– *expressing probability*

- ❑ I should think so.
- ❑ Probably.
- ❑ I'm pretty sure they will / would ...
- ❑ In all probability they will / would ...
- ❑ Almost certainly. / Almost definitely.
- ❑ Yes, I'm quite sure they would.

PROBLEMS

– *inquiring about problems*

- ❑ I was told that you could possibly help me.
- ❑ Do you have any idea where I can ...?
- ❑ Could you help me find ..., please?
- ❑ Excuse me. Could you help me, please? I'd like to ...

– *dealing with problems*

- ❑ What seems to be the problem?
- ❑ Can I help you in some way?
- ❑ I'll see what we can do for you.
- ❑ There seems to be a mistake somewhere.
- ❑ I'm afraid there's a little problem / mistake.
- ❑ We shall have to find a solution very quickly.
- ❑ Sorry about the mistake on our part.
- ❑ Let's see what we can work out, shall we?
- ❑ There's obviously been some sort of an oversight.
- ❑ I'll try and find out for you.
- ❑ We'll have it repaired immediately.
- ❑ We'll take care of it right away.
- ❑ I'll see to it immediately.
- ❑ Can I get back to you on this?
- ❑ I'm very sorry but I can't help you. Please contact ...

– *dealing with registration difficulties*

- ❑ My name's not on the list.
- ❑ I don't seem to be ...
- ❑ Excuse me. You've spelt / spelled my name wrong.
- ❑ For some reason you're not on ...
- ❑ Sorry, no. You don't appear anywhere.

PRODUCTS (see WORKPLACE, page 116)

PROPOSALS

– *making proposals*

- ❑ I propose that ...
- ❑ Well, I would propose that ...
- ❑ I would like to put forward a proposal that ...
- ❑ I hope you'll agree that ...
- ❑ Wouldn't it be better to ...?
- ❑ How about if ...?
- ❑ Well, don't you think we should ...?
- ❑ I suggest (most strongly) that ...
- ❑ I strongly recommend that ...
- ❑ Well, in my view the only viable solution is that ...

– *making neutral suggestions*

- ❑ How about ...?
- ❑ Shall we ...?
- ❑ Why don't we ...?
- ❑ Why not ...?
- ❑ Let's try ..., OK?
- ❑ We could ...
- ❑ I suggest we ...
- ❑ Supposing we ...
- ❑ How would you feel about ...?
- ❑ I wonder if I might suggest ...
- ❑ If I may make a suggestion ...
- ❑ We could always consider ...

– *expressing emphatic views*

- ❑ I particularly want to emphasize the fact that ...
- ❑ It is essential that ...
- ❑ I feel this is a vital issue.

- ❑ I consider this point to be of the utmost importance.

– *motioning*

- ❑ I propose that ...
- ❑ I would like to propose the motion that ...
- ❑ I would like to move that ...
- ❑ With the Chair's / Chairman's permission, I move that ...

PURPOSE

– *stating the purpose of a meeting*

- ❑ Before we begin I'd like to make a few remarks concerning ...
- ❑ The most important points seem to be ...
- ❑ Let me start by giving an outline of my proposals ...
- ❑ Our purpose in meeting here today is to discuss ...
- ❑ What we have to do this morning is ...
- ❑ By the end of this meeting we must have decided ...

– *explaining the purpose of a presentation*

- ❑ I'd like to talk about ...
- ❑ I'm here to present ...
- ❑ I shall be dealing with ...
- ❑ I'm here to tell you (all) about ...
- ❑ My purpose today is to talk about ...
- ❑ I'd like to just give you a brief breakdown of ...
- ❑ To start with, ... then ...
- ❑ Firstly, ... and secondly, ... and finally ...

Q

QUESTIONS

– *asking to speak to someone on the telephone*

- ❑ Could I talk to ..., please?
- ❑ Can I speak to ..., please?
- ❑ I'm trying to get hold of ...
- ❑ I'm trying to contact ... / to get in touch with ...
- ❑ Would / Could you put me through to ..., please?

– *asking for identification on the telephone*

- ❑ Who's calling, please?
- ❑ Who shall I say is calling?
- ❑ Yes, certainly. Could I have your name, please?
- ❑ Could I have your name again, please?
- ❑ Would you spell that for me, please?
- ❑ I wonder if you would mind spelling that for me, please.

– *asking for the phone*

- ❑ Where can I phone from?
- ❑ Is there a phone here I can use, please?
- ❑ Excuse me, is there a telephone here somewhere?
- ❑ Excuse me, does anybody know where there's a phone?
- ❑ Excuse me, could you tell me where I can find a telephone, please?

– *asking about hotel accommodation*

- ❑ Do you have any vacancies?
- ❑ I'd like to inquire about ...
- ❑ I'd like to make a reservation for ...
- ❑ I'd like to know the price of ...
- ❑ How much do you charge for a single / double room?
- ❑ Is breakfast included in the price?
- ❑ What credit cards do you take?

– *asking for directions*

- ❑ I'm looking for the ...
- ❑ How far is it to ... from here?
- ❑ Excuse me, is it a long way to ...?
- ❑ Excuse me, can you tell me the way to ..., please?
- ❑ Excuse me, can you tell me where ... is, please?
- ❑ Excuse me, could you tell me how to get to ..., please?
- ❑ Can you tell me where the ... is taking place?

– *asking for identification*

- ❑ Who shall I say is here?
- ❑ Can / May I have your name, please?
- ❑ What company are you from?
- ❑ Do you have an appointment?
- ❑ Who do you have an appointment with?

– *asking for clarification and further explanation*

- ❑ Excuse me, could you explain how ... is done?
- ❑ Excuse me, could you review ...?
- ❑ Could / Would you, please, explain this process?

- ❑ Would you mind briefly going over ...?
- ❑ I wonder if you could ...
- ❑ Just to make sure I've got it right ...
- ❑ Did I understand you correctly that ...?
- ❑ To go back to what you were saying about ...
- ❑ Sorry to interrupt, but I wonder if you could / would explain about ... again for me.
- ❑ Sorry to interrupt, but I didn't quite catch what you said about ...
- ❑ While you're on the topic of ..., may I ask ...?

– *asking for opinions*

- ❑ What do you think about / of ...?
- ❑ What's your opinion of ...?
- ❑ How do you feel about ...?
- ❑ How do you react to ...?
- ❑ What are your views on ...?
- ❑ I'd like to hear your views on ...

– *asking about someone*

- ❑ How's ...? / How are ...?
- ❑ Have you heard from ... lately?

– *asking for further information*

- ❑ Could you be a little more precise?
- ❑ Could you give us some details about ...?
- ❑ Could you expand on that?
- ❑ I'm sorry but could you explain in a little more detail?
- ❑ Would you care to elaborate on that?

– *asking someone to check information*

- ❑ Excuse me. Would you please check that ...?
- ❑ I'd like to make sure that ...
- ❑ Is it possible for you to find out whether (or not) ...?

– *asking for assistance*

- ❑ I wonder if you can help me.
- ❑ Do you think you could send this ... for me?
- ❑ Sorry to bother you, but would you mind ...?

– *asking for confirmation*

- ❑ Would I be correct in saying that ...?
- ❑ If I've understood correctly, you're saying that ...
- ❑ Am I correct in assuming that ...?
- ❑ Are you saying that ...?
- ❑ Basically, what you're saying is ...
- ❑ If you could, please confirm ...
- ❑ Could you send us confirmation by fax, please?

– *inquiring about problems*

- ❑ I was told that you could possibly help me.
- ❑ Do you have any idea where I can ...?
- ❑ Could you help me find ..., please?
- ❑ Excuse me. I sent a package of ... to this address ...

– *inquiring about arrangements*

- ❑ I'd just like to know whether it's possible to ...
- ❑ Who do I see to arrange...?
- ❑ To whom do I talk to arrange ...?
- ❑ Where do I sign up for ...?
- ❑ Where can I get ...?
- ❑ I need ... How can that be arranged?
- ❑ How can I get hold of ...?
- ❑ Where's ... being held?
- ❑ Can you tell me where ... is, please?

– *asking presenters questions*

- ❑ I was wondering if I understood correctly ...
- ❑ Referring to what you said about ...
- ❑ About what you said concerning ...
- ❑ I was wondering if I could ask something about ...

– *asking polite questions*

- ❑ Could you tell me ...?
- ❑ I wonder if you could tell me ...
- ❑ I wonder if ...
- ❑ Would you mind telling me how ...?
- ❑ Excuse me. Could you spare me a moment, please?
- ❑ Would you be good enough to tell me ...?
- ❑ May I ask ...?
- ❑ I was just wondering if I might ask ...
- ❑ I'd like to find out (about) ...

– *asking for repetition*

- ❑ I beg your pardon?
- ❑ What was that?
- ❑ How was that?
- ❑ What did you say?
- ❑ Come again?
- ❑ Sorry? What did you say?
- ❑ Pardon? I didn't quite get that.
- ❑ I'm afraid I didn't quite get that.
- ❑ Sorry. Could you repeat that, please?
- ❑ Sorry. Could you say that again, please?
- ❑ I'm sorry. I didn't quite follow what you said.
- ❑ I'm afraid I didn't catch your last point. Can you asking go over it again, please?
- ❑ I'm afraid I can't understand what you ...

– *asking for permission*

- ❑ Excuse me, may / can / could I ...?
- ❑ Do you think I could ...?
- ❑ I wonder if I could ...
- ❑ Is it all right if I ...?
- ❑ Do you mind if I ...?

– *asking general questions about a company*

- ❑ I wonder if you could give me some idea about / of the size of your company?
- ❑ Could you give me an idea of how many people are employed by your company?
- ❑ How many people do you have working in your company?
- ❑ How many countries do you export to?
- ❑ I'd be very much interested to hear what countries you export to.
- ❑ What kind of (a) network do you have in terms of scale?
- ❑ What exactly is your product range?
- ❑ Can I ask you about your product range?
- ❑ Do you specialize in any particular products?

– *asking about products*

- ❑ Could this model be used for ...?
- ❑ Is this model suitable for ...?
- ❑ Do you think this make could be used for ...?
- ❑ I'm interested in its technical specifications.
- ❑ How about its capacity?
- ❑ What about performance?
- ❑ Is this model available in different sizes?
- ❑ Is it possible for you to make tailor-made models?

- ❑ Do you think this series could be modified to suit ...?

– *requesting printed material*

- ❑ Do you have any brochures I could have?
- ❑ Have you got a brochure / leaflet / handout on it?
- ❑ Perhaps you might have some sales literature you could let me have?

– *asking tricky questions*

- ❑ I hope you don't mind me asking, but ...
- ❑ Have you ever taken into account...?
- ❑ I was just wondering if you'd thought of ...
- ❑ I can't help feeling ...
- ❑ I was wondering if ...
- ❑ Don't get me wrong, but ...

– *answering tricky questions*

- ❑ I'm not really sure, but ...
- ❑ I can't tell you off-hand, I'm afraid.
- ❑ I'll have to find out for you.
- ❑ I can let you know later, if you like.

– *avoiding the question*

- ❑ I'm afraid I'm not in a position to comment on that.
- ❑ Well, it's rather difficult to say at present.
- ❑ I'm afraid I don't have enough information at my disposal to answer that.

R

REASSURING

– *reassuring people*

- ❑ There's no danger of that.
- ❑ There's no cause for concern as far as ... is concerned.
- ❑ Let me assure you straight away on that point.
- ❑ I can assure you that ...
- ❑ We understand your concern about that and we can assure you that we will do everything in our power to ...

RECEPTIONIST

– *receiving a visitor*

- ❑ How can I help you?
- ❑ May I help you?
- ❑ What can I do for you?
- ❑ Can I help you?

– *asking for identification on the telephone*

- ❑ Who's calling, please?
- ❑ Who shall I say is calling?
- ❑ Could I have your name, please?
- ❑ Could I have your name again, please?
- ❑ Would you spell that for me, please?
- ❑ I wonder if you would mind spelling that for me, please.

– *asking for identification*

- ❑ Who shall I say is here?
- ❑ Can / May I have your name, please?
- ❑ What company are you from?

- ❑ Do you have an appointment?
- ❑ Who do you have an appointment with?

– *contacting the appropriate person and informing the visitor*

- ❑ Just one moment, please. I'll give him a call. I'll page him.
- ❑ Would you like to take a seat?
- ❑ He's expecting you.
- ❑ He'll be with you in a moment.
- ❑ I'm sorry. He's just stepped out for a while.
- ❑ He'll be right back.
- ❑ I'm sorry. He's not answering at the moment.
- ❑ I'll try again in a moment.
- ❑ I'm very sorry, but Mr / Ms ... is not here at the moment.
- ❑ Perhaps there's someone else who can help.

– *giving directions on the premises*

- ❑ Straight ahead, past the lifts / elevators, on your right.
- ❑ Take the first turning on the left.
- ❑ It's at the end of the corridor.
- ❑ Take the lift / elevator to the fifth floor.
- ❑ If you'd like to come with me I'll take you there.
- ❑ I'll get someone to show you the way.
- ❑ I'll try and get someone to help you.

– *giving messages*

- ❑ There's a message for you.
- ❑ A Ms ... was asking for you. She said she would try and get hold of you later.
- ❑ She said that she would phone back later.
- ❑ She couldn't wait for you any longer, but she did leave a message ...

– *dealing with registration difficulties*

- ❑ My name's not on the list.
- ❑ I don't seem to be ...
- ❑ Excuse me. You've spelt / spelled my name wrong.
- ❑ For some reason you're not on ...
- ❑ Sorry, no. You don't appear anywhere.

– *dealing with hotel reservations*

- ❑ A single or a double room?
- ❑ A single / double room costs ...
- ❑ When will you be arriving?
- ❑ And how many nights is it?
- ❑ How long will you be staying?
- ❑ What dates did you have in mind?
- ❑ How will you be paying?
- ❑ Thank you for your reservation.
- ❑ How will you be confirming your reservation?
- ❑ Will you send me the names by fax?
- ❑ We'll give you two weeks to confirm. OK?
- ❑ Could you give me your credit card number, please?

REFERRING

– *referring to something specific (on the telephone)*

- ❑ Referring to ...
- ❑ Did you get my fax about / concerning ...?
- ❑ I'm coming to ... so I was just wondering if ...
- ❑ You said in your letter last week that ...
- ❑ I did try a couple of times but your line was occupied / busy / engaged.

– *referring to future contacts*

- ❑ Well, if there's anything else you would like to know, give me a call later.
- ❑ We'll be delighted to give you all the help / assistance we can.
- ❑ We'll send you the info / brochures / price lists ... later.
- ❑ Well, look, if ever you're in ..., why don't you drop in and see us? I'd be delighted to show you around.
- ❑ I'm certain something will come (out) of this.

REFUSING (see also REJECTING)

– *refusing permission*

- ❑ No, I'm sorry.
- ❑ I'm afraid you can't.
- ❑ I'm sorry but you can't.
- ❑ Well, I'd rather you didn't if you don't mind.

REGARDS

– *sending regards*

- ❑ Love to ...
- ❑ Say hello to ...
- ❑ Remember me to ...
- ❑ Give my (very) best regards to ... (Thanks, I will.)

– *giving regards*

- ❑ Hello from ...
- ❑ (Best) regards from ...
- ❑ ... sends his / her regards.

REGISTERING

– *registering*

- ❑ Can you tell me where we register, please?
- ❑ How do I obtain ...?
- ❑ I'd like to pick up my registration pack.
- ❑ You wouldn't happen to have …?
- ❑ Would you please register at ...?
- ❑ Would you please fill in the registration form?

– *dealing with registration difficulties*

- ❑ My name's not on the list.
- ❑ I don't seem to be ...
- ❑ Excuse me. You've spelt / spelled my name wrong.
- ❑ For some reason you're not on ...
- ❑ Sorry no. You don't appear anywhere.

REJECTING

– *rejecting time and place*

- ❑ Sorry. I'm already booked.
- ❑ Sorry. That won't work.
- ❑ No. I'm sorry. That's no good.
- ❑ I'm afraid I've got something else on.
- ❑ Wait a minute. No, sorry. I've got something else then.

– *declining invitations*

- ❑ I'd love to but ...
- ❑ I'm awfully sorry but ...
- ❑ I'm afraid I can't ...
- ❑ It's really nice of you to ask, but ...
- ❑ Well, I hope you don't mind but ...
- ❑ I'd really like to but I'm afraid I can't.

- ❑ Sorry, no. We can't make it tonight. Maybe some other time.
- ❑ Sorry, no. I've already arranged to go somewhere else.

– *refusing drinks*

- ❑ Not for me, thank you.
- ❑ Not just yet. Maybe later.
- ❑ No more for me, thanks.
- ❑ No, thanks. I'm driving.
- ❑ No, thank you. I don't drink.

– *rejecting a compromise*

- ❑ I'm sorry I can't go along with that.
- ❑ No, I'm afraid it won't work.
- ❑ No, I'm afraid I still couldn't agree.
- ❑ I'm afraid it just wouldn't be feasible.
- ❑ We find your offer unacceptable.
- ❑ You leave us little alternative but to turn ... down.

– *rejecting suggestions*

- ❑ No, I don't think that's a good idea.
- ❑ I'd rather not if you don't mind.
- ❑ I'm afraid I couldn't go along with that.
- ❑ I don't know. I don't really like the sound of it very much.

REPETITION

– *asking for repetition*

- ❑ I beg your pardon?
- ❑ What was that?
- ❑ How was that?
- ❑ What did you say?
- ❑ Come again?
- ❑ Sorry? What did you say?
- ❑ Pardon? I didn't quite get that.

- ❑ I'm afraid I didn't quite get that.
- ❑ Sorry. Could you repeat that, please?
- ❑ Sorry. Could you say that again, please?
- ❑ I'm sorry. I didn't quite follow what you said.
- ❑ I'm afraid I didn't catch your last point. Can you go over it again, please?
- ❑ I'm afraid I can't understand what you ...

REPHRASING

– *rephrasing a point*

- ❑ Perhaps I haven't made myself clear.
- ❑ Basically, what I'm trying to say is ...
- ❑ Sorry. I'm probably not making myself clear.
- ❑ Let me put it another way.
- ❑ Allow me to rephrase that.
- ❑ To be more specific, ...
- ❑ Perhaps I should make that clear by saying ...

REPORTING

– *presenting group work*

- ❑ Our task was to ...
- ❑ The objective of our group was ...
- ❑ From the outset, our group ...
- ❑ The discussion then focused on ...
- ❑ This led to ...
- ❑ It was agreed that ...
- ❑ A number of points emerged from our discussion.
- ❑ We also stressed the ...
- ❑ We would like to underline the following points.
- ❑ This led us to make the following proposals.

- ❑ Lastly, the discussion turned to ...
- ❑ All in all, ...
- ❑ As far as our group is concerned, ...

REQUESTING

– *requesting printed material*

- ❑ Do you have any brochures I could have?
- ❑ Have you got a brochure / leaflet / handout on it?
- ❑ Perhaps you might have some sales literature you could let me have?

RESERVATION

– *expressing reservation*

- ❑ I can see what you mean, but ...
- ❑ Maybe, but don't you think ...?
- ❑ Don't you think we should also consider ...?
- ❑ That's true, but on the other hand ...
- ❑ But have you considered ...?
- ❑ I have certain reservations ...
- ❑ I'm rather worried about ...
- ❑ Under no circumstances should we come to a hasty decision on this.
- ❑ (However,) I can't help feeling that ...
- ❑ I feel that in view of ...

RESPONDING

– *responding to an invitation that has been declined*

- ❑ All right. Never mind.
- ❑ Some other time then.
- ❑ Oh dear. Well, I quite understand, of course.

– *responding to good news*

- ❑ Really?
- ❑ That's great news!
- ❑ Congratulations!
- ❑ That's great!
- ❑ You must be very pleased.
- ❑ Good. Glad to hear it.

– *responding to bad news*

- ❑ I'm very sorry to hear that.
- ❑ That *is* bad news.
- ❑ What a pity.
- ❑ That's a shame.

– *responding to questions from the audience*

- ❑ That's a good question.
- ❑ I'm glad you asked me that question.
- ❑ I thought someone would ask me about that.
- ❑ I'll have to give some thought to that.
- ❑ I'm not sure if I understood your question.
- ❑ I'm afraid I'm unable to answer your question.
- ❑ If I understood you correctly, ...

RESTAURANT

– *getting a table at a restaurant*

- ❑ A table for two, please.
- ❑ Good evening. We'd like a table for three, please.
- ❑ Good evening. We have a table reservation.
- ❑ Yes, sir / madam. What name, please?
- ❑ Just one moment, please.
- ❑ This way, please.

- ❑ Certainly, sir / madam. Would you care / like to follow me, please?

– deciding on food in a restaurant

- ❑ What about number four?
- ❑ What would you like?
- ❑ What shall we have to start with / to follow / to finish with?
- ❑ Can you tell me what ... is?
- ❑ Have you made your selection?
- ❑ Have you decided?
- ❑ Are you ready to order?
- ❑ What do you recommend?
- ❑ I'll have ... / I'd like ...

– addressing the waiter

- ❑ Can I have / see the menu, please?
- ❑ I wonder if you could help us.
- ❑ We're ready to order.
- ❑ Could I have the bill, please?

– complaints in a restaurant

- ❑ Excuse me, will it be much longer before we're served?
- ❑ Do you think we could change tables, please?
- ❑ Excuse me, this is not what I ordered.
- ❑ Excuse me, there's some mistake. This is not my order.
- ❑ Sorry to bother you but this ... is too ...

S

STARTING

– opening a formal meeting

- ❑ Ladies and gentlemen, I declare the meeting open.

- ❑ Let's get down to business, everyone, shall we?
- ❑ Let's get this meeting underway.
- ❑ Well, I think we all know why we're here.

– *opening a conference*

- ❑ It's my pleasure to welcome you all to the conference.
- ❑ It's my honour as the chairperson to declare this ... open.

– *opening an informal meeting*

- ❑ Let's get started, shall we?
- ❑ Let's get down to business, shall we?
- ❑ Let me start by ...
- ❑ I'd like to start by ...
- ❑ First of all ...
- ❑ To begin with ...
- ❑ I'd like to bring up the question of ...

– *starting a presentation*

- ❑ Good morning, ladies and gentlemen. Welcome to ...
- ❑ My name is ... and I'm a(n) ... with ...
- ❑ On behalf of ..., I'd like to welcome you all here to ...
- ❑ As you know, I'm here to present ... to you.
- ❑ Nice to see you all here.
- ❑ Let me begin by saying ...
- ❑ Let's start by looking at ...
- ❑ First I'd like to say a few words about ...
- ❑ I shall be dealing with ...
- ❑ I'm here to tell you (all) about ...

– *starting another point*

- ❑ Now I'd like to talk about ...
- ❑ Now I want to say a few words about ...
- ❑ Now I'd like to move on to ...

- ❑ Now I'd like to proceed by ...
- ❑ As you see, I now want to ...
- ❑ If I may, I'd now like to draw your attention to ...
- ❑ Next I'd like to concentrate on ...
- ❑ The next point I wish to deal with ...

– *starting group work*

- ❑ I suppose we'd better start by introducing ourselves.
- ❑ I think we should begin by ...
- ❑ This group is going to deal with ...
- ❑ We have to give a short report on ...
- ❑ Would anyone like to volunteer to serve as spokesperson?
- ❑ Would anyone like to volunteer to take the minutes?
- ❑ Who would like to take notes?
- ❑ Would anyone here like to represent this group?
- ❑ Who would like to report our conclusions?

SUGGESTIONS

– *making neutral suggestions*

- ❑ How about ...?
- ❑ Shall we ...?
- ❑ Why don't we ...?
- ❑ Why not ...?
- ❑ Let's try ..., OK?
- ❑ We could ...
- ❑ I suggest we ...
- ❑ Supposing we ...
- ❑ I wonder if I might suggest ...
- ❑ If I may make a suggestion ...
- ❑ How would you feel about ...?
- ❑ We could always consider ...

– *accepting suggestions*

- ❑ That's a good idea.
- ❑ All right.
- ❑ (It's) not a bad idea.
- ❑ Yes, I suppose we could.

– *rejecting suggestions*

- ❑ No, I don't think that's a good idea.
- ❑ I'd rather not if you don't mind.
- ❑ I'm afraid I couldn't go along with that.
- ❑ I don't know. I don't really like the sound of it very much.

– *making proposals*

- ❑ I propose that ...
- ❑ Well, I would propose that ...
- ❑ I would like to put forward a proposal that ...
- ❑ I hope you'll agree that ...
- ❑ Wouldn't it be better to ...?
- ❑ How about if ...?
- ❑ Well, don't you think we should ...?
- ❑ I suggest (most strongly) that ...
- ❑ I strongly recommend that ...
- ❑ Well, in my view the only viable solution is that ...

– *expressing emphatic views*

- ❑ It is essential that ...
- ❑ I particularly want to emphasize the fact that ...
- ❑ I feel this is a vital issue.
- ❑ I consider this point to be of the utmost importance.

– *motioning*

- ❑ I propose that ...

- ❑ I would like to propose the motion that ...
- ❑ I would like to move that ...
- ❑ With the Chair's / Chairman's permission, I move that ...

– *introducing a point*

- ❑ I'd like to bring up the point about ...
- ❑ I'd like to bring up the question of ...
- ❑ I'd like to mention briefly ...
- ❑ At this point, ...

– *suggesting you meet later*

- ❑ Well, perhaps we can arrange to meet later on tonight.
- ❑ Shall we all meet (up) later?
- ❑ Is there any chance of us meeting later?
- ❑ Well, what about this evening? Do you have anything planned?
- ❑ Well, if you're free, I'd like to offer you dinner ...
- ❑ How about in front of ... at ...?
- ❑ What time? 6? 7? Let's say 7.
- ❑ 8 o'clock. If that's all right with you?
- ❑ You suggest the place.

SUMMARIZING

– *summarizing*

- ❑ Well, if I could just sum up the discussion.
- ❑ To summarize, I think we're in agreement on ...
- ❑ To sum up, there seems to be ...
- ❑ So, in short, ...
- ❑ Well, if I may go over the main points raised so far ...,

T

TELEPHONING

– *answering the phone*

❑ Good morning. Can I help you?
❑ Hello. ... (company name)

– *asking to speak to someone on the telephone*

❑ Could I talk to ..., please?
❑ Can I speak to ..., please?
❑ I'm trying to get hold of ...
❑ I'm trying to contact ... / to get in touch with ...
❑ Would / Could you put me through to ..., please?

– *asking for identification on the telephone*

❑ Who's calling, please?
❑ Who shall I say is calling?
❑ Yes, certainly. Could I have your name, please?
❑ Could I have your name again, please?
❑ Would you spell that for me, please?
❑ I wonder if you would mind spelling that for me, please.

– *introducing yourself on the telephone*

❑ Hello. This is ... phoning from ...
❑ This is ... I'm calling from ...
❑ My name is ...
❑ Good morning. This is … from ...

– *ending a telephone conversation*

❑ Look forward to hearing from you then.

- ❑ I'm looking forward to meeting you.
- ❑ Thanks for calling. It's been nice talking to you.
- ❑ Nice talking to you, too.
- ❑ Fine. Hope to see you, on ...
- ❑ Thank you, see you then. Goodbye.
- ❑ If I don't hear from you ... I'll give you a call ...
- ❑ That's just about it for now. I'll get back to you later.

– *other key phrases for the telephone*

- ❑ Would you hold the line a moment, please?
- ❑ Would you wait a moment, please?
- ❑ Could you call back later?
- ❑ Shall I ask him to call you back?
- ❑ May I give him a message?
- ❑ Can you take a message?
- ❑ I'm sorry. The line is occupied / busy / engaged.
- ❑ I'm sorry. He's not answering at the moment.

– *asking for the phone*

- ❑ Where can I phone from?
- ❑ Is there a phone here I can use, please?
- ❑ Excuse me, is there a telephone here somewhere?
- ❑ Excuse me, does anybody know where there's a phone?
- ❑ Excuse me, could you tell me where I can find a telephone, please?

THANKING

– *thanking the visitors / the audience*

- ❑ Thank you for your attention, everyone.

❑ Thank you for your attention this afternoon.
❑ Thank you for listening to me.
❑ Thank you all for listening so patiently.

– *thanking the host*
❑ Thank you for a lovely evening.
❑ It's been a wonderful evening. Thank you very much.

– *thanking someone for assistance*
❑ Thank you very much (indeed) for your help.
❑ Thanks for your assistance.
❑ Thank you for helping me.
❑ I appreciate your help.
❑ Thank you. I'd appreciate it.

– *thanking the speaker*
❑ I'd like to thank ... for his very interesting talk and now move the discussion to the floor.
❑ Would anyone like to ask a question?
❑ Thank you. I'm sure you've given us a lot to think about.

– *thanking people for their interest*
❑ Yes, well, thank you very much indeed for giving me so much to think about.
❑ Thank you for a very interesting discussion.
❑ Thanks a lot for the information. I'm sure it'll prove very useful.

TIME

– *arranging time*
❑ Can we agree on a time?
❑ Shall we say ...?

- ❑ What day would be the most convenient ...?
- ❑ What day would suit you best?
- ❑ What time of day ...?
- ❑ How long do you think we'll need?
- ❑ When will you be arriving in ...?

– *accepting time and place*

- ❑ Fine with me.
- ❑ OK. Let's meet there.
- ❑ Suits me fine.
- ❑ I'll be there.
- ❑ I'll be waiting for you in / at ...
- ❑ Good. What time would be most suitable for you?
- ❑ Great. I'll come and pick you up at your hotel at ...

– *rejecting time and place*

- ❑ Sorry. I'm already booked.
- ❑ Sorry. That won't work.
- ❑ No. I'm sorry. That's no good.
- ❑ I'm afraid I've got something else on.
- ❑ Wait a minute. No, sorry. I've got something else then.

– *confirming time and place*

- ❑ So, we're meeting in ... on ... at ...
- ❑ Right, so it's ...
- ❑ Ten o'clock it is then.
- ❑ Just to confirm ...
- ❑ When you get here, all you have to do ...

– *suggesting you meet later*

- ❑ Well, perhaps we can arrange to meet later on tonight.
- ❑ Shall we all meet (up) later?
- ❑ Is there any chance of us meeting later?

- ❑ Well, what about this evening? Do you have anything planned?
- ❑ Well, if you're free, I'd like to offer you dinner ...
- ❑ How about in front of ... at ...?
- ❑ What time? 6? 7? Let's say 7.
- ❑ 8 o'clock. If that's all right with you?
- ❑ You suggest the place.

– *agreeing on meeting later*

- ❑ All right. What time and where?
- ❑ OK, shall we say at seven in the lobby?
- ❑ Yes, I don't see why not.
- ❑ OK, seven it is then. See you later.

TRAVELLING

– *making travel arrangements*

- ❑ I'd like to find out about ...
- ❑ Do you have any information on ...?
- ❑ I'm inquiring about ...
- ❑ I'd like a ... ticket to ..., please.
- ❑ Do I have to change?
- ❑ I'd like to book a ...
- ❑ I'd like to make a reservation, please?
- ❑ Do you accept credit cards?

– *making changes in travel arrangements*

- ❑ I'd like to make a change in my reservation.
- ❑ I'd like to change my ...
- ❑ Is it possible to exchange this ticket for ...?
- ❑ I'd like to cancel ...

U

UNCERTAINTY

– *expressing uncertainty*

❑ Well, it's possible, I suppose.
❑ Well, there might be a chance, yes.
❑ Yes, it could happen, I suppose.
❑ Well, there's always a chance, I suppose.
❑ I'm not really sure, but ...
❑ I can't tell you off-hand, I'm afraid.
❑ I'll have to find out for you.
❑ I can let you know later, if you like.

V

VISITORS (see also GUESTS)

– *receiving a visitor (receptionist)*

❑ How can I help you?
❑ May I help you?
❑ What can I do for you?

– *contacting the appropriate person and informing the visitor*

❑ Just one moment, please. I'll give him a call. / I'll page him.
❑ Would you like to take a seat?
❑ He's expecting you.
❑ He'll be with you in a moment.
❑ I'm sorry. He's just stepped out for a while.
❑ He'll be right back.
❑ I'm sorry. He's not answering at the moment.
❑ I'll try again in a moment.
❑ I'm very sorry, but Mr / Ms ... is not here at the moment.

- ❑ Perhaps there's someone else who can help.

– *welcoming visitors to your workplace*

- ❑ Glad you could join us today.
- ❑ We're very pleased to have you with us today.
- ❑ On behalf of ... I would like to welcome you all here today to ...

– *thanking the visitors / the audience*

- ❑ Thank you for your attention, everyone.
- ❑ Thank you for listening to me.
- ❑ Thank you all for listening so patiently.

VOTING

– *moving towards a vote*

- ❑ Perhaps we should take a formal vote on this.
- ❑ Let's put it to the vote.
- ❑ Could we take a vote on it?
- ❑ Can we move to vote on this?

– *the language of voting*

- ❑ Can I have a show of hands?
- ❑ Those *for* the motion, please?
- ❑ Will those in favour of the motion raise their right hands?
- ❑ Those against?
- ❑ Any abstentions?
- ❑ The motion is carried unanimously.
- ❑ The motion has been carried by six votes to five.
- ❑ The motion has been rejected / defeated by six votes to five.

WELCOMING

– *welcoming visitors to your workplace*

- ❑ Glad you could join us today.
- ❑ We're very pleased to have you with us today.
- ❑ On behalf of ... I would like to welcome you all here today to ...

– *making guests feel welcome*

- ❑ Hello. How are you?
- ❑ Glad you could make it.
- ❑ I'm so pleased you could come.
- ❑ Please come in and make yourself at home.
- ❑ Here, let me take your coat.
- ❑ May I take your coat?

– *welcoming participants to a conference*

- ❑ It's my pleasure to welcome you all to the conference.

WORKPLACE

– *giving directions on the premises*

- ❑ Straight ahead, past the lifts / elevators, on your right.
- ❑ Take the first turning on the left.
- ❑ It's at the end of the corridor.
- ❑ Take the lift / elevator to the fifth floor.
- ❑ If you'd like to come with me I'll take you there.
- ❑ I'll get someone to show you the way.
- ❑ I'll try and get someone to help you.

– *welcoming visitors to your workplace*

- ❑ We're very pleased to have you with us today.
- ❑ On behalf of ... I would like to welcome you all here today to ...
- ❑ Glad you could join us today.

– *introducing yourself and your workplace*

- ❑ My name is ... I'm ...
- ❑ As you know our job here mainly concerns ...
- ❑ I'm in charge of ...
- ❑ Here at ... we ...
- ❑ I'd like to show you the way we do things around here.

– *starting a workplace presentation*

- ❑ Before I start I'd just like to mention that ...
- ❑ Let's start by looking at ...
- ❑ First I'd like to say a few words about ...
- ❑ I shall be dealing with ...
- ❑ I'm here to tell you (all) about ...

– *asking general questions about a company*

- ❑ I wonder if you could give me some idea about the size of your company?
- ❑ Could you give me an idea of how many people are employed by your company?
- ❑ How many people do you have working in your company?
- ❑ How many countries do you export to?
- ❑ I'd be very much interested to hear what countries you export to.
- ❑ What kind of (a) network do you have in terms of scale?

- ❑ What exactly is your product range?
- ❑ Can I ask you about your product range?
- ❑ Do you specialize in any particular products?

– *asking about products*

- ❑ Could this model be used for ...?
- ❑ Is this model suitable for ...?
- ❑ Do you think this make could be used for ...?
- ❑ I'm interested in its technical specifications.
- ❑ How about its capacity?
- ❑ What about performance?
- ❑ Is this model available in different sizes?
- ❑ Is it possible for you to make tailor-made models?
- ❑ Do you think this series could be modified to suit ...?

– *requesting printed material*

- ❑ Do you have any brochures I could have?
- ❑ Have you got a brochure / leaflet / handout on it?
- ❑ Perhaps you might have some sales literature you could let me have?

– *referring to future contacts*

- ❑ Well, if there's anything else you would like to know about, give me a call later.
- ❑ We'll be delighted to give you all the assistance we can.
- ❑ We'll send you the info / brochures / price lists later.
- ❑ Well, look, if ever you're in ..., why don't you drop in and see us? I'd be delighted to show you around.
- ❑ I'm certain something will come (out) of this.

TARGET INDEX 2

2 "NICE TO MEET YOU"

– the language of making contact

7 "TO BE QUITE FRANK..."
– the language of negotiations

11.15 – *refusing permission*
11.16 – *answering tricky questions*
11.17 – *finding out identity*
11.18 – *thanking people for their interest*
11.19 – *referring to future contacts*
11.20 – *saying goodbye formally*

"I'm afraid I'm not in a position to comment on that."

PHRASE LIST 2:

TARGETS LISTED ACCORDING TO COURSE BOOK

"Did you get my fax?"

2

"NICE TO MEET YOU"

THE LANGUAGE OF MAKING CONTACT

2.1 – *answering the phone*

- ❑ Good morning. Can I help you?
- ❑ Hello. ... (company name)

2.2 – *asking to speak to someone on the telephone*

- ❑ Could I talk to ..., please?
- ❑ Can I speak to ..., please?
- ❑ I'm trying to get hold of ...
- ❑ I'm trying to contact ... / to get in touch with ...
- ❑ Would / Could you put me through to ..., please?

2.3 – *asking for identification on the telephone*

- ❑ Who's calling, please?
- ❑ Who shall I say is calling?
- ❑ Yes, certainly. Could I have your name, please?
- ❑ Could I have your name again, please?
- ❑ Would you spell that for me, please?
- ❑ I wonder if you would mind spelling that for me, please.

2.4 – *introducing yourself on the telephone*

- ❑ Hello, this is ... phoning from ...

- This is ... I'm calling from ...
- My name is ...
- Good morning / afternoon / evening. This is ... from ...

2.5 – *making an appointment*

- I'd like to make an appointment with ...
- Would it be possible to make an appointment with ...?
- I was wondering if it would be possible to make an appointment with ...?

2.6 – *referring to something specific (on the telephone)*

- Referring to ...
- Did you get my fax ...?
- I'm coming ... so I was just wondering if ...
- You said in your letter last week that ...
- I did try a couple of times but your line was occupied / busy / engaged.

2.7 – *arranging time*

- Can we agree on a time?
- Shall we say ...?
- What day would be the most convenient for you?
- What day would suit you best?
- What time of day ...?
- How long do you think we'll need?
- When will you be arriving in ...?

2.8 – *arranging place*

- Where should we meet?
- Let's meet at ...
- What about if we meet at ...? / What about meeting at ...?

- ❑ I suggest we meet at ... / Why don't we meet at ...?
- ❑ What's the address?
- ❑ Do you know the address?
- ❑ Do you know how to get here?
- ❑ Should I take a cab / taxi?
- ❑ Shall I pick you up at ...?
- ❑ Just to make sure I've got the time and place right ...

2.9 – *accepting time and place*

- ❑ Fine with me.
- ❑ OK. Let's meet there.
- ❑ Suits me fine.
- ❑ I'll be there.
- ❑ I'll be waiting for you in / at ...
- ❑ Good. What time would be most suitable for you?
- ❑ Great. I'll come and pick you up at your hotel at ...

2.10 – *rejecting time and place*

- ❑ Sorry. I'm already booked.
- ❑ Sorry. That won't work.
- ❑ No. I'm sorry. That's no good.
- ❑ I'm afraid I've got something else on.
- ❑ Wait a minute. No, sorry. I've got something else then.

2.11 – *confirming time and place*

- ❑ So, we're meeting in ... on ... at ...
- ❑ Right, so it's ...
- ❑ Ten o'clock it is then.
- ❑ Just to confirm ...
- ❑ When you get here, all you have to do ...

2.12 – *leaving things open*

- ❑ Let's leave it like that.
- ❑ Let's leave it open for the time being.
- ❑ Let's decide later, shall we?
- ❑ OK. I'll get back to you later on that.

2.13 – *ending a telephone conversation*

- ❑ Look forward to hearing from you then.
- ❑ I'm looking forward to meeting you.
- ❑ Thanks for calling. It's been nice talking to you.
- ❑ Nice talking to you, too.
- ❑ Fine. Hope to see you on ...
- ❑ Thank you, see you then. Goodbye.
- ❑ If I don't hear from you ... I'll give you a call ...
- ❑ That's just about it for now. I'll get back to you later.

2.14 – *asking about hotel accommodation*

- ❑ Do you have any vacancies?
- ❑ I'd like to inquire about ...
- ❑ I'd like to make a reservation for...
- ❑ I'd like to know the price of ...
- ❑ How much do you charge for a single / double room?
- ❑ Is breakfast included in the price?
- ❑ What credit cards do you take?

2.15 – *dealing with hotel reservations*

- ❑ A single or a double room?
- ❑ A single / double room costs ...
- ❑ When will you be arriving?
- ❑ And how many nights is it?
- ❑ How long will you be staying?
- ❑ What dates did you have in mind?

❑ How will you be paying?
❑ Thank you for your reservation.
❑ How will you be confirming your reservation?
❑ Will you send me the names by fax?
❑ We'll give you two weeks to confirm. OK?
❑ Could you give me your credit card number, please?

2.16 – *other key phrases for the telephone*

❑ Would you hold the line a moment, please?
❑ Would you wait a moment, please?
❑ Could you call back later?
❑ Shall I ask him to call you back?
❑ May I give him a message?
❑ Can you take a message?
❑ I'm sorry. The line is occupied / busy / engaged.

2.17 – *approaching others*

❑ Mr ... / Ms ...?
❑ It's ..., isn't it?
❑ Excuse me, are you ...?
❑ Hello, you must be ...

2.18 – *introducing oneself*

❑ Let me introduce myself. I'm ...
❑ Oh, I'm sorry. I haven't introduced myself. I'm ...

2.19 – *greeting people for the first time*

❑ Pleased to meet you. I'm ... from ...
❑ I'm ... Pleased to meet you.
❑ How do you do?
❑ Nice to meet you.
❑ I'm glad to meet you too.
❑ Kind of you to come and meet me.

❑ I've been looking forward to meeting you.

2.20 – *greeting an acquaintance*

❑ Hello, ... Good to see you again.
❑ Nice to see you again.
❑ Hello, ... How are you?
❑ Hi. How's it going?
❑ How are you keeping?
❑ How are things with you?
❑ What have you been up to since the last time we met?
❑ Oh, not so bad, you know. You?
❑ Well, I'm still alive.
❑ No complaints.
❑ Very well, thank you. How about you?
❑ Hi ... Pretty good, thanks. And you?
❑ All right. It's been some time. Nearly ...
❑ Really. Has it been that long?
❑ I'm so sorry, I can't quite remember your name.

2.21 – *introducing others*

❑ Can / May I introduce you to my colleague, Mr / Ms ...?
❑ ..., I'd like you to meet ... He / She works for ...
❑ Mr / Ms ..., please allow me to introduce you to ...
❑ ..., this is ... He's our ...
❑ I don't believe you two have met before, have you?
❑ This is ... from ... John Smith, our ...
❑ I'd like you all to meet my friend ...

2.22 – *suggesting you meet later*

❑ Well, perhaps we can arrange to meet later on tonight.

- ❑ Shall we all meet (up) later?
- ❑ Is there any chance of us meeting later?
- ❑ Well, what about this evening? Do you have anything planned?
- ❑ Well, if you're free, I'd like to offer you dinner ...
- ❑ How about in front of ... at ...?
- ❑ What time? 6? 7? Let's say 7.
- ❑ 8 o'clock. If that's all right with you?
- ❑ You suggest the place.

2.23 – *agreeing on meeting later*

- ❑ All right. What time and where?
- ❑ Shall we say at seven in the lobby?
- ❑ Yes, I don't see why not.
- ❑ OK, seven it is then. See you later.

2.24 – *taking your leave*

- ❑ I really should be going now.
- ❑ Well, I'm afraid I have to be going now.
- ❑ Well, it's been marvellous running into you like this.
- ❑ Nice seeing you, too.
- ❑ I really must be off now.
- ❑ Listen, I have to be getting along now.
- ❑ I'd better be going, too.
- ❑ Well, I really can't be staying any longer.
- ❑ Well, I'd better be going, I suppose.
- ❑ Well, it really is time I was off.
- ❑ Well, I think it's about time I started making my way home.
- ❑ Well, I really must be getting along.
- ❑ Well, I think I had better think about leaving.
- ❑ Oh, look at the time!

2.25 – *saying goodbye*

- ❑ Be seeing you. / So long.
- ❑ OK, see you then. / See you later.
- ❑ Sure, see you then.

"Well, it's been marvellous running into you like this."

3

"ON BEHALF OF OUR COMPANY..."

THE LANGUAGE OF RECEIVING VISITORS

3.1 – *asking for directions*

- ❑ I'm looking for the ...
- ❑ How far is it to ... from here?
- ❑ Excuse me, is it a long way to ...?
- ❑ Excuse me, can you tell me the way to ..., please?
- ❑ Excuse me, can you tell me where ... is, please?
- ❑ Excuse me, could you tell me how to get to ..., please?
- ❑ Can you tell me where the ... is taking place?

3.2 – *giving simple directions*

- ❑ Walk / Go down / along this street ...
- ❑ Walk straight on / ahead.
- ❑ Go straight on until you come to ... / as far as ...
- ❑ Turn right / left at ...
- ❑ Take the first turning right / left.
- ❑ It's not very far. / It's quite near here.
- ❑ It won't take you long.
- ❑ It's about ... minutes from here.
- ❑ It'll take you about ... minutes to get there.

3.3 – *receiving a visitor (receptionist)*

- ❑ How can I help you?
- ❑ May I help you?
- ❑ What can I do for you?

3.4 – *informing reception of your arrival*

- ❑ I have an appointment with Mr / Ms ... at ...
- ❑ I'm here from ...
- ❑ My name is ... I'm here to see ...
- ❑ I'm ... Can you tell me where ... is, please?

3.5 – *asking for identification*

- ❑ Who shall I say is here?
- ❑ Can / May I have your name, please?
- ❑ What company are you from?
- ❑ Do you have an appointment?
- ❑ Who do you have an appointment with?

3.6 – *contacting the appropriate person and informing the visitor*

- ❑ Just one moment, please. I'll give him a call. / I'll page him.
- ❑ Would you like to take a seat?
- ❑ He's expecting you.
- ❑ He'll be with you in a moment.
- ❑ I'm sorry. He's just stepped out for a while.
- ❑ He'll be right back.
- ❑ I'm sorry. He's not answering at the moment.
- ❑ I'll try again in a moment.
- ❑ I'm very sorry, but Mr / Ms ... is not here at the moment.
- ❑ Perhaps there's someone else who can help.

3.7 – *giving directions on the premises*

- ❑ Straight ahead, past the lifts / elevators, on your right.

- ❑ Take the first turning on the left.
- ❑ It's at the end of the corridor.
- ❑ Take the lift / elevator to the fifth floor.
- ❑ If you'd like to come with me I'll take you there.
- ❑ I'll get someone to show you the way.
- ❑ I'll try and get someone to help you.

3.8 – *asking about messages*

- ❑ My name's ... Do you have any messages for me?
- ❑ I'm expecting a message ...
- ❑ Were there any messages for me today?

3.9 – *leaving messages*

- ❑ I'd like to leave a message ...
- ❑ I'm expecting a phone call from ... If he phones could you ...?
- ❑ If anyone phones for me, would you please tell them ...

3.10 – *giving messages*

- ❑ There's a message for you.
- ❑ A Mr ... was asking for you. He said he would try and get hold of you later.
- ❑ He said that he would phone back later.
- ❑ He couldn't wait for you any longer, but he did leave a message ...

3.11 – *welcoming visitors to your workplace*

- ❑ Good morning, everyone.
- ❑ We're very pleased to have you with us today.
- ❑ On behalf of ... I would like to welcome you all here today to ...
- ❑ Glad you could join us today.

3.12 – *introducing yourself and your workplace*

- ❑ My name is ... I'm ...
- ❑ As you know our job here mainly concerns ...
- ❑ I'm in charge of ...
- ❑ Here at ... we ...
- ❑ I'd like to show you the way we do things around here.

3.13 – *starting a workplace presentation*

- ❑ Let's start by looking at ...
- ❑ Before I begin I'd just like to mention that ...
- ❑ First I'd like to say a few words about ...
- ❑ I shall be dealing with ...
- ❑ I'm here to tell you (all) about ...

3.14 – *asking for clarification and further explanation*

- ❑ Excuse me, could you explain how ... is done?
- ❑ Excuse me, could you review ...?
- ❑ Would you mind briefly going over ...?
- ❑ I wonder if you could ...
- ❑ Just to make sure I've got it right ...
- ❑ Sorry to interrupt, but I wonder if you could / would explain about ... again for me.
- ❑ Did I understand you correctly that ...?
- ❑ To go back to what you were saying about ...
- ❑ Could / Would you, please, explain this process?
- ❑ Sorry to interrupt, but I didn't quite catch what you said about ...

❑ While you're on the topic of ... may I ask ...?

3.15 – ***thanking the visitors / the audience***

❑ Thank you for your attention, everyone.

❑ Thank you for listening to me (so patiently).

"Thank you for your attention, everyone."

4

"THE FLOOR IS YOURS"
THE LANGUAGE OF FORMAL MEETINGS

4.1 – *opening a formal meeting*

- ❑ Ladies and gentlemen, I declare the meeting open.
- ❑ Let's get down to business, everyone, shall we?
- ❑ Let's get this meeting underway.
- ❑ Well, I think we all know why we're here.

4.2 – *stating the purpose of a meeting*

- ❑ The most important points seem to be ...
- ❑ Let me start by giving you an outline of my proposals ...
- ❑ Our purpose in meeting here today is to discuss ...
- ❑ What we have to do this morning is ...
- ❑ By the end of this meeting we must have decided ...
- ❑ Before we begin I'd like to make a few remarks concerning ...

4.3 – *dealing with the minutes*

- ❑ May I read the minutes?
- ❑ I'll read the minutes of the last meeting.
- ❑ It was decided that ...
- ❑ Would someone move that the minutes of the last meeting be accepted?

- ❑ We can take the minutes as being read.

4.4 – *dealing with the agenda*

- ❑ Has everyone seen the agenda?
- ❑ Has everyone received a copy of the agenda?
- ❑ Before we begin, I would like to add an item to the agenda.
- ❑ Referring to the agenda ...
- ❑ I would like to delete item five from the agenda.
- ❑ The agenda has been adopted.

4.5 – *giving someone the floor*

- ❑ Mr / Ms …, would you like to say something about this?
- ❑ At this point I'd like to give the floor to ...
- ❑ Mr ..., I think you know something about this. Perhaps I can bring you in here.
- ❑ Have you got anything to say about this, ...?
- ❑ Very well ... The floor is yours.
- ❑ The floor is open.

4.6 – *taking the floor*

- ❑ Mr Chairman, could I have the floor, please?
- ❑ Excuse me, Mr Chairman, may I say something, please?
- ❑ With the Chair's permission, I'd like to take up the point about ...

4.7 – *guiding the discussion*

- ❑ We seem to be losing sight of the main point.
- ❑ The question is ...
- ❑ This isn't relevant to our discussion.
- ❑ What we're trying to do is ...
- ❑ Could we keep / stick to the agenda, please?

4.8 – *keeping order*

- ❑ We can't all speak at the same time.
- ❑ Order! Order!
- ❑ Could we stick to the agenda, please?
- ❑ Mr / Ms ..., would you care to address your remarks to the Chair?

4.9 – *moving on to a new point (in a meeting)*

- ❑ Could we move on to item three on the agenda?
- ❑ Now I'd like to turn to ...
- ❑ Can we now go to ...?
- ❑ Has anyone anything further they would wish to add?

4.10 – *paging*

- ❑ Will Mr / Ms ..., please report to the ...?
- ❑ Will Mr / Ms ... kindly go to the ...?
- ❑ Paging Mr / Ms ...
- ❑ Oh, I'm just being paged. / I've just been paged.

4.11 – *excusing oneself*

- ❑ Excuse me a moment.
- ❑ I'm afraid I must leave you for a minute.
- ❑ I'll be right back.

4.12 – *asking for the phone*

- ❑ Where can I phone from?
- ❑ Is there a phone here I can use, please?
- ❑ Excuse me, is there a telephone here somewhere?
- ❑ Excuse me, does anybody know where there's a phone?
- ❑ Excuse me, could you tell me where I can find a telephone, please?

4.13 – *postponing*

- ❑ If no one has any objections, I suggest we leave this matter until our next meeting.
- ❑ Well, ladies and gentlemen, with your approval, I propose to defer this matter until ...

4.14 – *motioning*

- ❑ With the Chair's / Chairman's permission, I move that ...
- ❑ I would like to move that ...
- ❑ I propose that ...
- ❑ I would like to propose the motion that ...

4.15 – *seconding a motion*

- ❑ Would anyone like to second the motion?
- ❑ Anyone wish to second that motion?
- ❑ Seconded! / I'll second that motion.
- ❑ Seconded by Mr / Ms ...

4.16 – *moving towards a vote*

- ❑ Perhaps we should take a formal vote on this.
- ❑ Let's put it to the vote.
- ❑ Could we take a vote on it?
- ❑ Can we move to vote on this?

4.17 – *the language of voting*

- ❑ Those *for* the motion, please?
- ❑ Will those in favour of the motion raise their right hands?
- ❑ Those against?
- ❑ Any abstentions?
- ❑ Can I have a show of hands?
- ❑ The motion is carried unanimously.
- ❑ The motion has been carried by six votes to five.

- ❑ The motion has been rejected / defeated by six votes to five.

4.18 – *consensus*

- ❑ It would seem we have a consensus.
- ❑ Can I take it everyone's in favour?
- ❑ Are we all agreed on that?
- ❑ Well, it looks as if we're basically in agreement on this.

4.19 – *closing a formal meeting*

- ❑ Is there any other business?
- ❑ Any further points?
- ❑ Is there anything else to discuss?
- ❑ I declare this meeting closed.
- ❑ If nobody has any further business, I think we can conclude the meeting for today.

"Well, I did say that the floor was open!"

5

"WHAT DO YOU THINK?"

THE LANGUAGE OF INFORMAL MEETINGS

5.1 – *opening an informal meeting*

- ❑ Let's get started, shall we?
- ❑ Let's get down to business, shall we?
- ❑ First of all ...
- ❑ To begin with ...
- ❑ Let me start by ...
- ❑ I'd like to start by ...

5.2 – *introducing a point*

- ❑ I'd like to bring up the point about ...
- ❑ I'd like to bring up the question of ...
- ❑ I'd like to mention briefly ...
- ❑ At this point ...

5.3 – *adding*

- ❑ I must add that ...
- ❑ In addition ...
- ❑ Not only ... but ...
- ❑ Furthermore ... / Moreover ...

5.4 – *giving examples*

- ❑ Let me give you an example.
- ❑ One example might be ...
- ❑ To illustrate this point ...

5.5 – *balancing*

- ❑ On the one hand, ... but on the other ...

- ❑ Although ... we mustn't forget ...
- ❑ In spite of ... / Despite ... I still think ...

5.6 – *generalizing*

- ❑ But on the whole ...
- ❑ In general ... / Generally speaking, ...
- ❑ All in all, ... / All things considered, ...

5.7 – *stating preferences*

- ❑ I'd rather ... than ...
- ❑ I'd rather not ...
- ❑ I prefer ... to ...

5.8 – *asking for opinions*

- ❑ What do you think about / of ...?
- ❑ What's your opinion of ...?
- ❑ How do you feel about ...?
- ❑ How do you react to ...?
- ❑ What are your views on ...?
- ❑ I'd like to hear your views on ...

5.9 – *giving opinions*

- ❑ I think / feel that ...
- ❑ In my opinion ...
- ❑ As I see it, ...
- ❑ I (firmly) believe that ...
- ❑ It's my belief / opinion that ...
- ❑ From my point of view, ...
- ❑ As far as I am concerned, ...

5.10 – *giving tentative opinions*

- ❑ It seems to me that ...
- ❑ I would say that ...
- ❑ As far as I'm able to judge ...
- ❑ I think it would be fair to say that ...

5.11 – *expressing strong agreement*

- ❑ I totally agree.

- I agree with you completely.
- I agree with you on that.
- That's exactly my opinion.
- I think you're right.
- I couldn't agree more.
- I'm all in favour of that.
- You're absolutely right.

5.12 – *expressing strong disagreement*

- (I'm sorry, but) I totally disagree with you.
- (I'm sorry, but) I don't agree with you (at all).
- (I'm sorry, but) I disagree entirely.
- Well, I (really) can't agree with you on that.
- No, I don't agree at all.
- You're completely mistaken.
- Under no circumstances could I agree to that.
- What you're saying is just not feasible.
- No way.
- I can't accept your point of view.
- I'm sorry, but that's really out of the question.
- To be quite frank, ...
- To put it bluntly, ...
- With respect, ...

5.13 – *expressing reservation*

- I can see what you mean, but ...
- Maybe, but don't you think ...?
- Don't you think we should also consider ...?
- That's true, but on the other hand ...
- But have you considered ...?
- I have certain reservations ...
- I'm rather worried about ...
- Under no circumstances should we come to a hasty decision on this.

- ❑ (However,) I can't help feeling that ...
- ❑ I feel that in view of ...

5.14 – *asking tricky questions*

- ❑ I hope you don't mind me asking, but ...
- ❑ Have you ever taken into account ...?
- ❑ I was just wondering if you'd thought of ...
- ❑ I can't help feeling ...
- ❑ I was wondering if ...
- ❑ Don't get me wrong, but ...

5.15 – *making neutral suggestions*

- ❑ How about ...?
- ❑ Shall we ...?
- ❑ Why don't we ...?
- ❑ Why not ...?
- ❑ Let's try ..., OK?
- ❑ We could ...
- ❑ I suggest we ...
- ❑ Supposing we ...
- ❑ How would you feel about ...?
- ❑ I wonder if I might suggest ...
- ❑ If I may make a suggestion, ...
- ❑ We could always consider ...

5.16 – *accepting suggestions*

- ❑ That's a good idea.
- ❑ All right.
- ❑ It's not a bad idea.
- ❑ Yes, I suppose we could.

5.17 – *rejecting suggestions*

- ❑ No, I don't think that's a good idea.
- ❑ I'd rather not if you don't mind.
- ❑ I don't know. I don't really like the sound of it very much.
- ❑ I'm afraid I couldn't go along with that.

5.18 – *expressing positive hesitation*

- ❑ Um ... well, actually ...
- ❑ How shall I put it?
- ❑ Well, in fact ... you see ...

5.19 – *avoiding the question*

- ❑ I'm afraid I'm not in a position to comment on that.
- ❑ Well, it's rather difficult to say at present.
- ❑ I'm afraid I don't have enough information at my disposal to answer that.

5.20 – *rounding up (an informal meeting)*

- ❑ Well, I think that covers everything.
- ❑ That just about wraps it up, I think.
- ❑ I think that's all we have time for.
- ❑ Can we leave it at that, for now?
- ❑ Let's finish it here, everyone.
- ❑ Let's call it a day, shall we?
- ❑ If there's nothing else, I suggest we finish.
- ❑ Perhaps we can finish by ...
- ❑ That's all for today. Thank you.

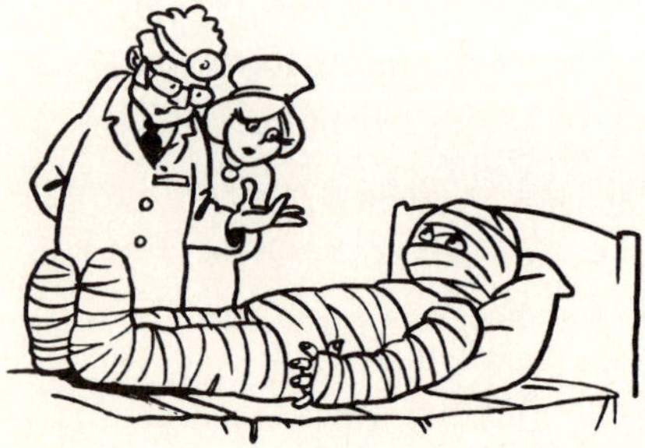

"That just about wraps things up, I think."

6

"BE MY GUEST"

THE LANGUAGE OF SOCIALIZING

6.1 – *inviting people*

- ❑ Would you like to ...?
- ❑ Would you care to ...?
- ❑ I was wondering if you would like to ...
- ❑ I was wondering if you would care to come to ...
- ❑ I was wondering if you would like to join me for ...
- ❑ How about going ...?
- ❑ Do you feel like spending the evening …?

6.2 – *accepting invitations*

- ❑ I'd love to.
- ❑ I'd be delighted to.
- ❑ Yes. I'd like to very much. Thanks.
- ❑ That's very kind of you. I'd like that very much.
- ❑ That would be very nice.
- ❑ Sounds like a great idea.

6.3 – *declining invitations*

- ❑ I'd love to but ...
- ❑ I'm awfully sorry but ...
- ❑ I'm afraid I can't.
- ❑ It's really nice of you to ask, but ...
- ❑ Well, I hope you don't mind but ...
- ❑ I'd really like to but I'm afraid I can't.

- ❑ Sorry, no. We can't make it tonight. Maybe some other time.
- ❑ Sorry, no. I've already arranged to go somewhere else.

6.4 – *responding to an invitation that has been declined*

- ❑ All right. Never mind.
- ❑ Some other time then.
- ❑ Oh dear. Well, I quite understand, of course.

6.5 – *making guests feel welcome*

- ❑ Hello. How are you?
- ❑ Glad you could make it.
- ❑ I'm so pleased you could come.
- ❑ Please come in and make yourself at home.
- ❑ Here, let me take your coat.
- ❑ May I take your coat?

6.6 – *asking about someone*

- ❑ How's ... / How are ...?
- ❑ Have you heard from ... lately?

6.7 – *breaking good news*

- ❑ Guess what?
- ❑ Did you know that ...?
- ❑ Have you heard that …?
- ❑ Good news, everyone!

6.8 – *responding to good news*

- ❑ Really?
- ❑ That's great news!
- ❑ Congratulations!
- ❑ That's great!
- ❑ You must be very pleased.
- ❑ Good. Glad to hear it.

6.9 – *breaking bad news*

- ❑ Bad news, I'm afraid.
- ❑ I've got some bad news for you, I'm afraid.

6.10 – *responding to bad news*

- ❑ I'm very sorry to hear that.
- ❑ That *is* bad news.
- ❑ What a pity.
- ❑ That's a shame.

6.11 – *informing people about the meal*

- ❑ Dinner will be ready in a minute.
- ❑ I think we're ready to begin serving dinner.
- ❑ Sorry to interrupt, but dinner is ready / served.

6.12 – *offering drinks*

- ❑ Would you like a drink?
- ❑ What would you like to drink?
- ❑ Drink, anyone?
- ❑ Can I get you a drink?
- ❑ What are you having?

6.13 – *accepting drinks*

- ❑ Thank you. I'll have a ...
- ❑ Thank you very much. I'll have a ..., please.
- ❑ Thank you. What do you recommend?
- ❑ I'd love one.

6.14 – *refusing drinks*

- ❑ Not for me, thank you.
- ❑ Not just yet. Maybe later.
- ❑ No more for me, thanks.
- ❑ No, thanks. I'm driving.
- ❑ No, thank you. I don't drink.

6.15 – *getting a table at a restaurant*

- ❑ A table for two, please.

- ❑ Good evening. We'd like a table for three, please.
- ❑ Good evening. We have a table reservation.
- ❑ Yes, sir / madam. What name, please?
- ❑ Just one moment, please.
- ❑ This way, please.
- ❑ Certainly, sir / madam. Would you care / like to follow me, please?

6.16 – *deciding on food in a restaurant*

- ❑ What about number four?
- ❑ What would you like?
- ❑ What shall we have to start with / to follow / to finish with?
- ❑ Well, the ... sounds delicious, doesn't it?
- ❑ That sounds very nice.
- ❑ Can you tell me what ... is?
- ❑ Have you made your selection?
- ❑ Have you decided?
- ❑ Are you ready to order?
- ❑ What do you recommend?
- ❑ I'll have ... / I'd like ...

6.17 – *addressing the waiter*

- ❑ Can I have / see the menu, please?
- ❑ I wonder if you could help us.
- ❑ We're ready to order.
- ❑ Could I have the bill, please?

6.18 – *table talk*

- ❑ Could you pass me the ..., please?
- ❑ Can I pass you the ...?
- ❑ Would you like (some) ...?

6.19 – *sending regards*

- ❑ Love to ....
- ❑ Say hello to ...

- ❑ Remember me to ...
- ❑ Give my (very) best regards to ... (Thanks, I will.)

6.20 – ***giving regards***

- ❑ Hello from ...
- ❑ (Best) regards from ...
- ❑ ... sends his / her regards.

6.21 – ***thanking the host***

- ❑ Thank you for a lovely evening.
- ❑ It's been a wonderful evening. Thank you very much.

"May I take your coat?"

7

"TO BE QUITE FRANK..."
THE LANGUAGE OF NEGOTIATIONS

7.1 – *making proposals*

- ❑ I propose that ...
- ❑ Well, I would propose that ...
- ❑ I would like to put forward a proposal that ...
- ❑ I hope you'll agree that ...
- ❑ Wouldn't it be better to ...?
- ❑ How about if ...?
- ❑ Well, don't you think we should ...?
- ❑ I suggest (most strongly) that ...
- ❑ I strongly recommend that ...
- ❑ Well, in my view the only viable solution is that ...

7.2 – *expressing partial agreement*

- ❑ Well, I agree with you on the whole, but ...
- ❑ I agree in principle, but ...
- ❑ Although I agree with most of what you've said, I ...
- ❑ I find it difficult to agree with your point about ...
- ❑ By and large I would accept your views, but ...
- ❑ Well, to a certain extent I agree with you, but ...
- ❑ You have a point there, but ...

- I have some sympathy with your position, but ...
- I take your point, but ...
- I can see your point of view, but ...

7.3 – *expressing neutral disagreement*

- Do you really think so?
- I can't say I share your view.
- I'm not totally convinced by your argument.
- I feel I must disagree.
- We'll have to agree to differ.
- Well, I can't help feeling that ...
- Well, personally I think that ...
- I don't know about that.
- I'm not so sure I agree with you.
- I wouldn't say that.
- I respect your opinion, of course; however ...
- Well, I can't say I'm completely happy with the idea.

7.4 – *adding information*

- There are certain points you should bear in mind.
- If we look at it in another light ...
- There are other considerations ...
- I wonder if you've considered ...
- Seen from another angle, one could ...
- Let me elaborate ...
- I'll explain it in greater detail.

7.5 – *asking for further information*

- Could you expand on that?
- Could you be a little more precise?
- Could you give us some details about...?
- I'm sorry but could you explain in a little more detail?

❑ Would you care to elaborate on that?

7.6 – *asking for confirmation*

❑ Would I be correct in saying that ...?
❑ If I've understood correctly, you're saying that ...
❑ Am I correct in assuming that ...?
❑ Are you saying that ...?
❑ Basically, what you're saying is ...
❑ If you could, please, confirm ...
❑ Could you send us confirmation by fax, please?

7.7 – *correcting misunderstandings*

❑ I'm afraid there seems to be a slight misunderstanding.
❑ We seem to be talking at cross purposes.
❑ I think you've misunderstood me / us.
❑ I'm afraid I haven't made myself clear enough.
❑ That isn't quite what I said.
❑ With all due respect, that's not what I said.

7.8 – *rephrasing a point*

❑ Perhaps I haven't made myself clear.
❑ Sorry, I'm probably not making myself clear.
❑ Let me put it another way.
❑ Allow me to rephrase that.
❑ To be more specific, ...
❑ Basically, what I'm trying to say is ...
❑ Perhaps I should make that clear by saying ...

7.9 – *reassuring people*

❑ There's no danger of that.
❑ There's no cause for concern as far as ... is concerned.

- ❑ Let me assure you straight away on that point.
- ❑ I can assure you that ...
- ❑ We understand your concern about that and we can assure you that we will do everything in our power to ...

7.10 – *expressing emphatic views*

- ❑ I particularly want to emphasize the fact that ...
- ❑ It is essential that ...
- ❑ I feel this is a vital issue.
- ❑ I consider this point to be of the utmost importance.

7.11 – *playing down a point*

- ❑ OK. But this is a minor issue.
- ❑ Yes, but this is only of secondary importance.
- ❑ Perhaps. But this, after all, is a relatively small point.

7.12 – *playing for time*

- ❑ That's a very interesting question.
- ❑ That's a difficult question to answer.
- ❑ I'm glad you asked that question.
- ❑ You have raised an important point there.
- ❑ I'm sure you will appreciate how complicated this matter is.
- ❑ Well, it's rather difficult to say at present.
- ❑ I'm afraid I don't have enough information at my disposal to answer that.
- ❑ I'm afraid I'm not in a position to comment on that just yet.

7.13 – *challenging a point of view*

- ❑ I wonder if that view is justified in the light of ...

- I don't think you fully appreciate the fact that ...
- It would be in your own interest to consider the matter in view of ...
- If I were you, I would be inclined to consider the matter in view of ...

7.14 – *offering a compromise*

- Is that acceptable as a compromise solution?
- We're prepared to ... provided ...
- I think we could ... on condition that ...
- We're ready to ... on the understanding that ...
- We're more than ready to ... as long as ...

7.15 – *accepting a compromise*

- That seems to be a reasonable compromise.
- Yes. I think that would be perfectly acceptable.
- We would have no objections to that.
- To meet you halfway on this, I think we could agree to your condition.

7.16 – *rejecting a compromise*

- I'm sorry I can't go along with that.
- No, I'm afraid it won't work.
- No, I'm afraid I still couldn't agree.
- I'm afraid it just wouldn't be feasible.
- We find your offer unacceptable.
- You leave us little alternative but to turn ... down.

7.17 – *summarizing*

- Well, if I could just sum up the discussion.
- To summarize, I think we're in agreement on ...

- ❑ To sum up, there seems to be ...
- ❑ So, in short ...
- ❑ Well, if I may go over the main points raised so far ...

7.18 – *concluding (negotiations)*

- ❑ Let me conclude by saying ...
- ❑ I'd like to conclude by stating that ...
- ❑ Allow me to conclude by highlighting the fact that ...
- ❑ In conclusion, I would like to reiterate ...
- ❑ I would now like to conclude my comments by assuring you that we are fully aware of the fact that ...

"You have a point there."

8

"CLEARLY AND SIMPLY"
THE LANGUAGE OF PRESENTATIONS

8.1 – *getting attention for a presentation*

- ❑ OK. Can I have your attention, everyone?
- ❑ OK. Are we ready?
- ❑ All right, everyone!
- ❑ So, ladies and gentlemen.
- ❑ Let's start, shall we?
- ❑ Let's get underway, shall we?

8.2 – *starting a presentation*

- ❑ Good morning, ladies and gentlemen. Welcome to ...
- ❑ As you know, I'm here to present ... to you.
- ❑ My name is ... and I'm a(n) ... with ...
- ❑ On behalf of ..., I'd like to welcome you all here to ...
- ❑ Nice to see you all here.
- ❑ Let me begin by saying ...

8.3 – *explaining the purpose of a presentation*

- ❑ I'd like to talk about ...
- ❑ I'm here to present ...
- ❑ My purpose today is to talk about ...
- ❑ I'd like to just give you a brief breakdown of ...

- ❑ To start with ..., then ...
- ❑ Firstly, ... and secondly, ... and finally...

8.4 – *drawing attention to a point*

- ❑ I think it's very significant that ...
- ❑ As you have noticed, ...
- ❑ As you can see, ...
- ❑ So you will, no doubt, see instantly that ...
- ❑ I'd now like to draw your attention to ...

8.5 – *finishing a point*

- ❑ OK. So much for ...
- ❑ That's all I'm going to say about ...
- ❑ And that's all I have to say about ...
- ❑ So that's ...
- ❑ OK. So we've looked at ...

8.6 – *starting another point*

- ❑ Now I'd like to talk about ...
- ❑ Now I want to say a few words about ...
- ❑ Now I'd like to move on to ...
- ❑ Now I'd like to proceed by ...
- ❑ As you see, I now want to ...
- ❑ If I may, I'd now like to draw your attention to ...
- ❑ Next I'd like to concentrate on ...
- ❑ The next point I wish to deal with ...

8.7 – *digressing during a presentation*

- ❑ Please allow me to digress for a while.
- ❑ If you let me, I'd like to digress for a while.
- ❑ I'd just like to mention in passing that ...

- ❑ But that's really a side issue. Let me return to what I was saying about ...
- ❑ Let me get back to my main point.
- ❑ To return to my original ...

8.8 – *ending a presentation*

- ❑ Let me end by saying that ...
- ❑ I'd like to finish by ...
- ❑ I think I've spoken long enough now, so ...
- ❑ Well, that's it (really).
- ❑ Well, that completes my end of things.
- ❑ So, to sum up, ... Thank you for your attention, ...
- ❑ It's been a pleasure to ...
- ❑ I hope you enjoyed ... / found it ...
- ❑ If you have any questions I'll do my best to answer them.

"If you have any questions I'll do my best to answer them."

9

"NO PROBLEM!"
THE LANGUAGE OF DEALING WITH DIFFICULTIES

9.1 – *informing someone about changes in schedule*

- ❑ The original schedule has been updated.
- ❑ There is a slight change in the schedule.
- ❑ Before we begin, I would like to announce that ... , which means there's a slight change in the schedule.
- ❑ I think we must postpone ... until ...
- ❑ The ... has been postponed until ...
- ❑ Mr / Ms ...'s presentation has been moved to ...
- ❑ The room assignments have been changed.
- ❑ ..., scheduled to be held in ..., will now be meeting in ...
- ❑ Due to technical reasons the ... has been cancelled.
- ❑ Due to unforeseen circumstances ...
- ❑ Due to circumstances beyond our control ...
- ❑ Apologies from Mr / Ms ... Unfortunately he / she won't be able to participate.

9.2 – *making changes in travel arrangements*

- ❑ I'd like to make a change in my reservation.
- ❑ I'd like to change my ...

- ❑ Is it possible to exchange this ticket for ...?
- ❑ I'd like to cancel ...

9.3 – *inquiring about problems*

- ❑ I was told that you could possibly / perhaps help me.
- ❑ Do you have any idea where I can ...?
- ❑ Excuse me. Could you help me, please. I'd like to ...
- ❑ Could you help me find ..., please?

9.4 – *asking someone to check information*

- ❑ Excuse me. Would you please check that ...?
- ❑ Is it possible for you to find out whether (or not) ...?
- ❑ I'd like to make sure that ...
- ❑ I'd just like to make sure that you've received ...

9.5 – *checking information*

- ❑ Just a moment, please. I'll have a look on the computer.
- ❑ I'm sorry. We have no record of your order.
- ❑ I'll have to check if we have a record of it.
- ❑ I'm sorry but we have no trace of it.
- ❑ Sorry, you don't appear on our ...
- ❑ Just a moment. I'll look up the details.
- ❑ I'll track this information down for you.
- ❑ I think we'd better get back to you on this one.

9.6 – *dealing with problems*

- ❑ What seems to be the problem?
- ❑ Can I help you in some way?
- ❑ I'll see what we can do for you.
- ❑ There seems to be a mistake somewhere.

- ❑ I'm afraid there's a little problem / mistake.
- ❑ We shall have to find a solution very quickly.
- ❑ Sorry about the mistake on our part.
- ❑ Let's see what we can work out, shall we?
- ❑ There's obviously been some sort of an oversight.
- ❑ I'll try and find out for you.
- ❑ Can I get back to you on this?
- ❑ I'm very sorry but I can't help you. Please contact ...
- ❑ We'll have it repaired immediately.
- ❑ We'll take care of it right away.
- ❑ I'll see to it immediately.

9.7 – *making polite complaints*

- ❑ I don't like to complain but …
- ❑ I'm sorry to complain but ...
- ❑ Excuse me but I really feel I have to complain ...
- ❑ Excuse me a moment. I'm afraid ...
- ❑ To whom can I make a complaint?
- ❑ I've got a problem with ...
- ❑ Excuse me, the ... doesn't work properly.
- ❑ I'd like to return this ...
- ❑ Could you possibly change my room?

9.8 – *thanking someone for assistance*

- ❑ Thank you very much (indeed) for your help.
- ❑ Thanks for your assistance.
- ❑ Thank you for helping me.
- ❑ I appreciate your help.
- ❑ Thank you. I'd appreciate it.

9.9 – *complaints in a restaurant*

- ❑ Excuse me, this is not what I ordered.

- ❑ Excuse me, there's some mistake. This is not my order.
- ❑ Sorry to bother you but this ... is too ...
- ❑ Excuse me, will it be much longer before we're served?
- ❑ Do you think we could change tables, please?

9.10 – *apologizing*

- ❑ I'm terribly / awfully / really sorry but I'm afraid ...
- ❑ Sorry about ...
- ❑ It's entirely our fault.
- ❑ Sorry about all this.
- ❑ Is there anything I can do?
- ❑ Please accept my apologies.
- ❑ I'm sorry. If there's anything I can do ...

"Excuse me, will it be much longer before we're served?"

10

"YOUR ATTENTION, PLEASE!"

THE LANGUAGE OF CONFERENCES

10.1 – *making travel arrangements*

- ❑ I'd like to find out about ...
- ❑ Do you have any information on ...?
- ❑ I'm inquiring about ...
- ❑ I'd like a ... ticket to ..., please.
- ❑ Do I have to change?
- ❑ I'd like to make a reservation, please.
- ❑ I'd like to book a ...
- ❑ Do you accept credit cards?

10.2 – *registering*

- ❑ Can you tell me where we register, please?
- ❑ How do I obtain ...?
- ❑ I'd like to pick up my registration pack.
- ❑ You wouldn't happen to have ...?
- ❑ Would you please register at ...?
- ❑ Would you please fill in the registration form?

10.3 – *dealing with registration difficulties*

- ❑ My name's not on the list.
- ❑ I don't seem to be ...
- ❑ Excuse me. You've spelt / spelled my name wrong.

- ❑ For some reason you're not on ...
- ❑ Sorry, no. You don't appear anywhere.

10.4 – *opening a conference*

- ❑ It's my pleasure to welcome you all to the conference.
- ❑ It's my honour as the chairperson to declare this ... open.
- ❑ It's my privilege to chair this session.

10.5 – *introducing the speaker*

- ❑ It's my pleasure to introduce our first speaker, ..., who will be talking about ...
- ❑ Our next speaker is ..., who will speak about ...
- ❑ The title of our next talk is ..., given by ... from ...

10.6 – *offering assistance*

- ❑ Can I help you in some way?
- ❑ May I be of assistance?
- ❑ Would you like me to do it for you?
- ❑ Can I give you a hand?

10.7 – *asking for assistance*

- ❑ I wonder if you can help me?
- ❑ Do you think you could send this ... for me?
- ❑ Sorry to bother you, but would you mind ...?

10.8 – *inquiring about arrangements*

- ❑ I'd just like to know whether it's possible to ...
- ❑ To whom do I talk to arrange ...?
- ❑ Who do I see to arrange ...?
- ❑ Where do I sign up for ...?
- ❑ Where can I get ...?
- ❑ I need ... How can that be arranged?

- ❑ How can I get hold of ...?
- ❑ Where's ... being held?
- ❑ Can you tell me where ... is, please?

10.9 – *starting group work*

- ❑ I suppose we'd better start by introducing ourselves.
- ❑ This group is going to deal with ...
- ❑ We have to give a short report on ...
- ❑ I think we should begin by ...
- ❑ Would anyone like to volunteer to serve as spokesperson?
- ❑ Would anyone like to volunteer to take the minutes?
- ❑ Who would like to take notes?
- ❑ Would anyone here like to represent this group?
- ❑ Who would like to report our conclusions?

10.10 – *presenting group work*

- ❑ Our task was to ...
- ❑ The objective of our group was ...
- ❑ From the outset, our group ...
- ❑ The discussion then focused on ...
- ❑ This led to ...
- ❑ It was agreed that ...
- ❑ A number of points emerged from our discussion.
- ❑ We also stressed the ...
- ❑ We would like to underline the following points.
- ❑ This led us to make the following proposals.
- ❑ Lastly, the discussion turned to ...
- ❑ All in all, ...
- ❑ As far as our group is concerned, ...

10.11 – *asking presenters questions*

- ❑ I was wondering if I understood correctly ...
- ❑ Thank you for an interesting presentation. Referring to what you said about ...
- ❑ About what you said concerning ...
- ❑ I was wondering if I could ask something about …

10.12 – *responding to questions from the audience*

- ❑ That's a good question.
- ❑ I'm glad you asked me that question.
- ❑ I thought someone would ask me about that.
- ❑ I'll have to give some thought to that.
- ❑ I'm not sure if I understood your question.
- ❑ I'm afraid I'm unable to answer your question.
- ❑ If I understood you correctly ...
- ❑ Maybe it would be better if we had a word afterwards.

10.13 – *thanking the speaker*

- ❑ I'd like to thank ... for his very interesting talk and now move the discussion to the floor.
- ❑ Would anyone like to ask the speaker a question?
- ❑ Thank you. I'm sure you've given us a lot to think about.

"Sorry, no. You don't appear anywhere."

11

"THANKS FOR THE INFORMATION"

THE LANGUAGE OF FAIRS

11.1 – *confirming arrangements*

- ❑ I'd just like to make sure you've received our ...
- ❑ I just wanted to make sure everything's in order.
- ❑ I'm phoning about ...
- ❑ You haven't made it clear to us ...
- ❑ Could you send us confirmation by fax?

11.2 – *asking general questions about a company*

- ❑ I wonder if you could give me some idea about the size of your company?
- ❑ Could you give me an idea of how many people are employed by your company?
- ❑ How many people do you have working in your company?
- ❑ How many countries do you export to?
- ❑ I'd be very much interested to hear what countries you export to.
- ❑ What kind of (a) network do you have in terms of scale?
- ❑ What exactly is your product range?
- ❑ Can I ask you about your product range?

- ❑ Do you specialize in any particular products?

11.3 – *asking about products*

- ❑ Could this model be used for ...?
- ❑ Is this model suitable for ...?
- ❑ Do you think this make could be used for ...?
- ❑ I'm interested in its technical specifications.
- ❑ How about its capacity?
- ❑ What about performance?
- ❑ Is this model available in different sizes?
- ❑ Is it possible for you to make tailor-made models?
- ❑ Do you think this series could be modified to suit ...?

11.4 – *requesting printed material*

- ❑ Do you have any brochures I could have?
- ❑ Have you got a brochure / leaflet / handout on it?
- ❑ Perhaps you might have some sales literature you could let me have?

11.5 – *asking polite questions*

- ❑ Excuse me. Could you spare me a moment, please?
- ❑ I'd like to find out (about) ...
- ❑ Could you tell me ...?
- ❑ I wonder if you could tell me ...
- ❑ Would you mind telling me how ...?
- ❑ Would you be good enough to tell me...?
- ❑ May I ask ...?
- ❑ I was just wondering if I might ask ...

11.6 – *asking for repetition*

- ❑ Sorry? What did you say?

- ❑ Pardon? I didn't quite get that.
- ❑ I'm afraid I didn't quite get that.
- ❑ Sorry. Could you repeat that, please?
- ❑ Sorry. Could you say that again, please?
- ❑ I beg your pardon?
- ❑ What was that?
- ❑ How was that?
- ❑ What did you say?
- ❑ Come again?
- ❑ I'm sorry. I didn't quite follow what you said.
- ❑ I'm afraid I didn't catch your last point. Can you go over it again, please?
- ❑ I'm afraid I can't understand what you ...

11.7 – *expressing certainty*

- ❑ Oh, yes, I'm absolutely sure ...
- ❑ I'm quite sure ...
- ❑ I'm certain ...
- ❑ I'm positive it will ...
- ❑ Yes. Definitely.
- ❑ Without a doubt.
- ❑ Absolutely. / Certainly.
- ❑ No, I'm absolutely sure ... (it isn't) ...
- ❑ No, I'm quite sure ... (it isn't) ...
- ❑ No, definitely not.
- ❑ Certainly not. / Absolutely not.

11.8 – *expressing probability*

- ❑ I should think so.
- ❑ Probably.
- ❑ I'm pretty sure they will / would ...
- ❑ In all probability they will / would ...
- ❑ Almost certainly. / Almost definitely.
- ❑ Yes, I'm quite sure they would.

11.9 – ***expressing improbability***

- ❑ I don't think so.
- ❑ Probably not.
- ❑ No, I'm sure it wouldn't.
- ❑ The chances are, it wouldn't.
- ❑ It's highly unlikely.
- ❑ There's very little chance of that happening.

11.10 – ***expressing uncertainty***

- ❑ Well, it's possible, I suppose.
- ❑ Well, there might be a chance, yes.
- ❑ Yes, it could happen, I suppose.
- ❑ Well, there's always a chance, I suppose.

11.11 – ***expressing doubt***

- ❑ Well, you never know, of course.
- ❑ No one can say for sure.
- ❑ Possibly. / Perhaps. / Maybe.
- ❑ I wouldn't like to say for sure.
- ❑ I'm not really sure.
- ❑ I doubt it.
- ❑ I have my doubts.
- ❑ It's doubtful.
- ❑ It's highly unlikely.

11.12 – ***expressing ignorance***

- ❑ I really wouldn't like to say.
- ❑ I must admit, I don't know.
- ❑ I've really no idea.
- ❑ I really couldn't say.
- ❑ I haven't a clue.
- ❑ I don't have the slightest idea.

11.13 – ***asking for permission***

- ❑ Excuse me, may / can / could I ...?
- ❑ Do you think I could ...?

- ❑ I wonder if I could ...
- ❑ Is it all right if I ...?
- ❑ Do you mind if I ...?

11.14 – *granting permission*

- ❑ Sure. / Certainly. / Yes, of course.
- ❑ Of course you can / may.
- ❑ Yes, by all means.
- ❑ Please, do.
- ❑ Go ahead.

11.15 – *refusing permission*

- ❑ No, I'm sorry.
- ❑ I'm afraid you can't.
- ❑ I'm sorry but you can't.
- ❑ Well, I'd rather you didn't if you don't mind.

11.16 – *answering tricky questions*

- ❑ I'm not really sure, but ...
- ❑ I can't tell you off-hand, I'm afraid.
- ❑ I'll have to find out for you.
- ❑ I can let you know later, if you like.

11.17 – *finding out identity*

- ❑ Excuse me but I didn't quite catch your name.
- ❑ Excuse me, what was your name again?
- ❑ I'm sorry, what company did you say you worked for / represented?
- ❑ If you'd just give me your name and address, I'll make sure you get all the information you want as soon as possible.
- ❑ If I could just have your name in the / our visitors' book?

11.18 – *thanking people for their interest*

- ❑ Yes well, thank you very much indeed for giving me so much to think about.

- Thank you for a very interesting discussion.
- Thanks a lot for the information. I'm sure it'll prove very useful.

11.19 – *referring to future contacts*

- Well, if there's anything else you would like to know, why not give me a call later?
- We'll be delighted to give all the help / assistance we can.
- We'll send you the info / brochures / price lists later.
- Well, look, if ever you're in ..., why don't you drop in and see us? I'd be delighted to show you around.
- I'm certain something will come (out) of this.

11.20 – *saying goodbye formally*

- Well, I hope we meet again in the very near future.
- I look forward to hearing from you soon.
- I look forward to seeing you in / at ...
- I look forward to receiving your offer / price list.
- Nice talking to you. Thank you so much.

"I'm certain something will come out of this."